ACRL Monograph Number 29

THE CAREER OF THE
ACADEMIC LIBRARIAN

A Study of the Social Origins, Educational Attainments,
Vocational Experience, and Personality Characteristics
of a Group of American Academic Librarians

By
PERRY D. MORRISON
School of Librarianship
University of Oregon

AMERICAN LIBRARY ASSOCIATION
Chicago 1969

ASSOCIATION OF COLLEGE AND
RESEARCH LIBRARIES MONOGRAPHS

Editor   David W. Heron
           University of Kansas

Editorial Board   J. Periam Danton
                    University of California (Berkeley)

                    Louis Shores
                    2013 West Randolph Circle
                    Tallahassee, Florida

                    Eileen Thornton
                    Oberlin College

                    Howard W. Winger
                    University of Chicago

Standard Book Number 8389-3089-1 (1969)
The Library of Congress card number
for the ACRL Monograph Series is 52-4228.
The card number of this title is 68-24079.

Acknowledgments

    This is a revised and condensed version of a dissertation submitted in partial satisfaction of the requirements for the degree of Doctor of Library Science at the University of California, Berkeley. I wish to thank the following professors who served on the advisory committee for the project during the course of the preparation of this study: J. Periam Danton, Ray E. Held, Thomas R. McConnell, LeRoy C. Merritt, Philip Selznick, James C. Stone, and Martin A. Trow. Other members of the faculties of the School of Education and the School of Librarianship were also most helpful, particularly Miss Marjorie Fiske. I am also indebted to Dr. Lyman W. Porter, of the Department of Psychology, for information about the Ghiselli Inventory. (Professor Ghiselli was on leave at the time the study was designed.)
    I have also received much help from the University of Oregon, Eugene. Dr. Carl W. Hintz, University Librarian, has given me much valuable guidance and encouragement. A number of other members of the faculty and staff also gave advice and assistance. Among these are Dr. Leona Tyler, of the Psychology Department (now Dean of the Graduate School); Dr. Robert Dubin, of the Sociology Department; Dr. Paul Civin, of the Department of Mathematics; and, especially, Mr. V. M. Sandor, IBM Supervisor, Business Office.
    I am further indebted to the University of Oregon for granting me two years' leave of absence in which to pursue advanced studies toward the degree of Doctor of Library Science, and to the Graduate School of the University and its former Dean, Dr. Harry A. Alpert (now Dean of Faculties), for the research grant which enabled me to prepare this revised version of the study.
    In connection with the supplementary chapter on developments since 1960, I am grateful for the support and encouragement of Dean

iv   Acknowledgments

LeRoy C. Merritt, of the School of Librarianship, University of Oregon, and for the assistance of Mr. William Snyder, Graduate Assistant.

I am doubly indebted to the aforementioned Professor J. Periam Danton; the fact that the study is now being published is due to his faith and perseverance.

My debt is very great, indeed, to the 707 librarians who took the time to give thoughtful consideration to a lengthy questionnaire and thus provide the basic data for the study.

Finally, there is the invaluable assistance of my wife, Catherine J. Morrison, to whom this study is dedicated.

PERRY D. MORRISON

Eugene, Oregon

Contents

Tables	vii
I. BACKGROUND AND DESCRIPTION OF THE SURVEY	1
Objectives	1
Methodology	2
II. SOCIAL, ECONOMIC, AND DEMOGRAPHIC ORIGINS	5
Social Origins and Economic Backgrounds	5
Educational Level of Parents	9
Geographic Origins	10
Summary	13
III. EDUCATION AND TRAINING	15
Undergraduate Education	15
Opinions about Undergraduate Education	21
Graduate Education	23
Advanced Subject Degrees	24
Professional Education for Librarianship	27
Advanced Degrees in Library Science	33
Opinions concerning Education for Librarianship	35
Summary	39
IV. CAREER FACTORS	43
Decision To Become a Librarian	43
Motivation for Entering Librarianship	47
"Anticipatory Socialization": Summary and Comment	51
In-service Factors	53
Obtaining a Position	54

Variety of Experience	55
Participation in Voluntary Associations	59
Publish or Perish?	63
Reaction to Library Work	65
Summary	74

V. PSYCHOLOGICAL CHARACTERISTICS ... 79

Self-Description Inventory	79
Evaluation of Responses	83
Interrelationship of Personality with Other Factors	89
Summary	93

VI. IMPLICATIONS OF FINDINGS ... 97

Social Characteristics	100
Education for Librarianship	102
Career Factors	107
The Librarian's Personality	118
Summary	122

VII. DEVELOPMENTS SINCE 1960 ... 125

APPENDICES

I. Questionnaire and Other Instruments Used in Gathering Data	139
II. Statistical Treatment	146
III. Suggestions for Further Research	149

BIBLIOGRAPHY (to 1960) ... 152

Tables

1.	Social Class Origins of Subjects Related to Age	6
2.	Father's Occupation for Seven Professional Groups	7
3.	Level of Father's Occupation	9
4.	Geographic Distribution of Subjects at Time of Survey	11
5.	Size of Undergraduate Alma Mater	16
6.	Size of Undergraduate Alma Mater—By Sex	16
7.	Size of Undergraduate Alma Mater Related to Salary—By Sex	17
8.	Type of Undergraduate Alma Mater	18
9.	Major Subject of Undergraduate Education	19
10.	Opinions concerning the Main Purposes of a College Education	22
11.	Highest Degrees Held by Subjects	24
12.	Possession of Master's Degree in an Academic Subject Related to Position Level and Salary	25
13.	Possession of Master's Degree in an Academic Subject Related to Position Level and Sex	25
14.	Type of Library School Attended	28
15.	Type of Library School Attended Related to Salary in 1958	29
16.	Reputation of Various Library Schools	30
17.	Possession of Old-Style Master's Degree in Library Science Related to Sex	33
18.	Salary Related to Possession of Old-Style Master's Degree by Sex	34
19.	Opinions concerning Objectives of Instruction in Library Science	36
20.	Time of First Consideration of Librarianship as a Career	44

viii   Tables

21.	Time of Final Choice of Librarianship as a Career	45
22.	Age at Entering Librarianship	46
23.	Contacts with Libraries Reported as Influencing Choice of Librarianship as a Career	47
24.	Reasons for Choosing Librarianship as a Career—By Sex	49
25.	Help Received by Subjects in Obtaining Positions in Libraries	54
26.	Mobility: Number of Libraries in Which Subjects Have Held Full-Time Positions—Related to Position and Sex	57
27.	Activity in Professional and Scholarly Organizations	59
28.	Activity in Professional and Scholarly Organizations Related to Salary	60
29.	Activity in Community Organizations	62
30.	Number of Publications	64
31.	Factors Liked Best about Library Work	67
32.	Factors Liked Least about Library Work	70
33.	Mean Scores on Ghiselli Self-Description Inventory Expressed as Percentiles of the Adult Employed Population	80
34.	Personality Traits: Mean Scores on the Ghiselli Self-Description Inventory	81
35.	Scores on Ghiselli Self-Description Inventory—By Sex	87
36.	Occupational Level Scores on Ghiselli Inventory Related to Salary	88
37.	Topics Chosen for Free Comment	99
38.	Father's Occupations for Academic, Public, and School Librarians and for Teachers' College Students	131
39.	Academic Attainments of Chief Librarians in Two Separate Studies	132

CHAPTER I

Background and Description of the Survey

The yearning for self-knowledge is endemic in mankind. One manifestation of this is a hunger on the part of the individual for information about the characteristics of the group of which he is a part and about the place of that group in society. The aim of this study is to supply this sort of information to academic librarians.

OBJECTIVES

It is to be expected that this information may be of some use to individuals in planning their lives; to the professional group as a whole in selecting, recruiting, and training new members; and to personnel administrators in developing the staffs of academic libraries.[1] However, the primary purpose is not utilitarian. Rather it is to discover sociological and psychological trends among academic librarians so that these librarians may better understand themselves and their relationship to the social order.

In attempting to furnish this type of information, this survey is simply following in the tradition of a number of previous studies of librarians and of members of other professional groups. Specifically, it follows in the tradition of the Public Library Inquiry which stated its mission as follows:

> The Inquiry can offer no rules of thumb by which the inadequacies of personnel revealed... can be eliminated. The studies, however, may help to clarify the personnel problem by presenting reliable information about the present personnel, its management, and its training. The volume as a whole will, we hope, provide a body of data upon which constructive policy can be based. It is intended to reveal the librarians to themselves.[2]

1

2   The Career of the Academic Librarian

In a more restricted way, the present study attempts to do for academic librarians what the personnel studies of the Public Library Inquiry did for public librarians in 1952, that is, to present "a picture of the people now employed as professional workers ... their personal characteristics, family backgrounds, education, interests, attitudes, and motivations...."[3]

To be more specific, this survey was designed to fill the following omissions in the body of knowledge about academic librarians: (1) How do college and university librarians compare with public librarians and with other professional people? (2) What characteristics tend to distinguish academic librarians holding one kind or level of position from others? and (3) What sequence of events seems to produce librarians for various types of positions in the profession?

METHODOLOGY

Before proceeding further, the reader should be warned that the method used to gather data in answer to the questions posed above was that of the survey in one point in time, rather than a "before and after" study. Thus, the effect of the passage of time can only be inferred, not directly observed. Secondly, lack of adequate definition of what constitutes true success in this, or any, profession puts undue emphasis upon such external and evanescent criteria as hierarchical position and salary. Objective information about these material achievements can be easily obtained, whereas data about more subtle contributions are very difficult to come by. Finally, previous research has shown that the process of producing that complex bundle of skills and ideals known as "professional man" is not simple. The hope of finding a simple index for predicting success in any profession is foredoomed.[4] Not only are the background factors in the career of the professional man complex, but also the requirements for "success" vary with the specific position a person occupies in his group.

As in other studies of professional people, the focus of this study is upon an elite group of librarians, i.e., the head librarians of American colleges and universities who earned $6000 or more in the year 1958. However, unlike many other studies, this survey gathered data from a sample of ordinary practitioners for comparison with those from the elite group.

The primary group, known as the "major executives," is composed of all of the head librarians earning $6000 a year or more for service in the 413 libraries reporting statistics for 1956-57 to the Association of College and Research Libraries. This group consisted of 231 librarians (84 percent of those to whom questionnaires were sent).

Background and Description of the Survey

The group of "ordinary" academic librarians was selected from the 1955 edition of *Who's Who in Library Service*. This sample, to be referred to hereafter as the "control group," numbered 476 (a 76 percent return from the questionnaire mailing). Members of this group are from the same sample of libraries as the major executives and were selected so that their average age was approximately the same (fifty years) as that of the major executives. Because of this matching for age, the control group was older, on the average, than academic librarians generally. Furthermore, because the information in *Who's Who in Library Service* was five years old in 1958, members of the control group had had at least five years' experience in library work at the time of the survey.

After the questionnaires were returned, the control group was divided into two subgroups on the basis of the number and type of personnel supervised. This made it possible to compare data for three groups of similar size:

1. Major executives (231): These are heads of college and university libraries earning $6000 or more in 1958.
2. Minor executives (232): Most of these are "middle managers," i.e., department heads, heads of branches, or section chiefs.
3. Others (244): These are librarians without extensive supervisory responsibilities.

The questionnaire used to gather information was distributed by mail. It consisted of (1) a section requesting information about personal history and statements of opinion about the state of librarianship, and (2) a standard "Self-Description Inventory" prepared by Edwin E. Ghiselli, of the University of California, for use in industrial personnel work.

A total of 707 subjects returned usable information (78.3 percent), a response which compares well with that reported by the Public Library Inquiry and by other surveys of professional groups. As far as can be determined, the general characteristics of those who returned questionnaires differed little from those who did not. However, it should be borne in mind that this is not a random sample of academic librarians generally. It is restricted to those working in libraries reporting to the Association of College and Research Libraries, to those who were sufficiently interested in their profession to respond to both the questionnaire of *Who's Who in Library Service* and to the present survey, and finally to those who had been in service at least five years. It is at least reasonable to speculate that such librarians are, on the average, more mature and energetic than those not included in the study. On the other hand, a few very vigorous individualists who believe social surveys to be nonsense have excluded themselves.

NOTES

[1] cf. Kenneth R. Shaffer, "Personnel and the Library School," *Library Trends*, 3:13 (July 1954).

[2] Alice I. Bryan, *The Public Librarian: A Report of the Public Library Inquiry* (New York: Columbia Univ. Press, 1952), p.12.

[3] *Ibid.*, p.3.

[4] cf. Eugene H. Wilson, "Pre-Professional Backgrounds of Students in a Library School," *Library Quarterly* 8:157-88 (April 1938), and J. Periam Danton and LeRoy C. Merritt, "Characteristics of the Graduates of the University of California School of Librarianship" (Univ. of Illinois Library School, "Occasional Papers," No.22, June 1951. Mimeographed).

CHAPTER II

Social, Economic, and Demographic Origins

It is the intention of this chapter to explore a few illustrations of the relationship between the economic and social order in twentieth-century America and the composition of the professional staff in American academic libraries.

SOCIAL ORIGINS AND ECONOMIC BACKGROUNDS

It has been repeatedly shown that one's occupation is a good index of the position he holds in society, an index of the "social honor" achieved.[1] A number of scales have been devised for translating occupational descriptions into social-status terms. Each has its advantages and limitations. The one used here was devised by W. Lloyd Warner and his associates to classify occupations according to the social status usually accorded to each.[2] From data supplied in the questionnaire about the occupation of subjects' fathers, the librarians were classified as coming from relatively high (Warner classes 1-3) or low (classes 4-7) status homes. Inasmuch as Warner classifies professional librarians as belonging to class 2, people who come into librarianship from classes 4-7 have undergone what sociologists call "upward mobility."

The following tabulation shows the social-class origins of subjects as indicated by their fathers' occupations. Figures are percentages and the classification is derived from Warner's revised scale:

	Upper classes (1-3)	Lower classes (4-7)
Major executives	69	31
Minor executives	76	24
Others	78	22

5

It can be seen from the tabulation that approximately three fourths of the subjects came into the profession from a social stratum not much lower nor higher than that occupied by librarians generally. That is to say, they "inherited" their fathers' occupational level.

However, comparisons among the three groups of subjects reveal that once a person has entered the library profession, lower-class origin is not a bar to rising in it. To the contrary, there appears to be some tendency for members of the major executive group to have come from lower-status families more frequently than those in the control group. This points to the conclusion that for a significant number of subjects, the energy that enabled a person to break the social barriers to entrance into the profession also tended to carry him upward within it.

Further analysis, not shown here, indicates that the above conclusion holds for members of each sex considered separately. However, there are some differences when the subjects are tabulated by age, as in Table 1. Among the young there is a greater

TABLE 1.
SOCIAL CLASS ORIGINS OF SUBJECTS RELATED TO AGE*

Social Class	Age Less than 50			Age Greater than 50		
	Major Executives (118)	Control Group (193)	Total (311)	Major Executives (103)	Control Group (262)	Total (365)
Upper classes (1-3)	64%	73%	70%†	76%	81%	79%
Lower classes	36	27	30	24	19	21

*Information lacking for 31 subjects.
†Difference between the younger and older totals significant at .01 level.

proportion of librarians from lower-class origin than there is among their elders. This indicates that the barriers are being lowered. More people from humble origins have been able to secure the education necessary and to meet the other requirements for entry into librarianship since 1930 than did so before. Also, the tendency for those from lower-class families to become head librarians is greater for the younger than for the older group. This indicates that a modest tendency for "democracy," in the sense of social mobility, is increasing in academic librarianship. To meet its needs for personnel, librarianship is dipping into the pool of talent in the lower classes of society. The spread of educational opportunity and, probably, the opportunity for persons of all classes to become acquainted with the world of books through the public library have made this possible. Incidentally, this tendency does not mean that the relative status of librarianship as an occupation is falling in prestige. The same tendencies are found in other professions such as medicine and law.[3]

Before becoming too sanguine about the opportunities available to a person who enters librarianship from a lower-class background, one should consider the additional fact that the concentration of such persons is in the lower-paid group of major executives. Of this group, 39 percent are from lower-class homes, whereas the proportion both for the higher-paid major executives and for the control group is 23 percent. A person whose father's occupation was of relatively low prestige enjoyed an advantage in achieving a position as head librarian of, say, a teachers' college, but his chances of rising to the most lucrative positions of the large universities seem not to have been affected one way or the other by his father's social status.

Classification of the occupation of one's father by type of work done, rather than by social class, throws additional light on the nature of the family backgrounds from which librarians come. The tabulation in Table 2 compares the type of occupation of fathers for seven groups of professional people.[4] "White collar" occupations include managerial and clerical workers, and "blue collar" indicates manual, service, or agricultural pursuits.

TABLE 2.
FATHER'S OCCUPATION FOR SEVEN PROFESSIONAL GROUPS

Occupational Group	Father's Occupation		
	Professional	White Collar	Blue Collar
Academic librarians (1958)	29%	41%	30%
Library science students (1948)	26	40	34
Eminent scientists (1946)	46	23	31
Business leaders (1952)*	14	60	24
Teachers' college students (1929)†	8	54	64
Psychologists (1954)*	42	34	21
Social work students (1954)	24	49	27

*"Other" or "not given": 2% for business leaders and 1% for psychologists.

†For undisclosed reasons proportions add up to 126%; probably two or more occupations were included for some subjects, whereas in other studies only "principal" occupation was included.

It will be noted that the data for the two studies of librarians are strikingly similar and that both the scientists and the psychologists are of higher-status social origin than are the librarians. From this it can be argued that, during the period covered, librarianship was frequently considered to be a white-collar occupation rather than a full profession, compared, that is, to a career in science requiring the doctorate or equivalent training.

Fewer schoolteachers than librarians are from families of professional men. A note on the data given above is in order here: Although the student teachers were queried in 1929 and the academic librarians in 1958, a moment's reflection will reveal that the average date of birth for both groups is about the same (1908-9).[5] Other studies have also shown that teaching tends to attract its candidates largely from the lower middle classes rather than from the families of professional people.[6] This leads to a speculation that differences in social-class backgrounds between teachers and librarians may partially explain why many persons who are unhappy, or even unsuccessful, schoolteachers may become happy, and successful, librarians. More research on this point is indicated even though the mind recoils from this kind of hypothesis!

As one would expect, fewer business leaders than librarians or scientists come from the families of professional men and relatively more from clerical and managerial backgrounds. However, business, science, and other professions are fishing in much the same pool of leadership talent as librarianship. The professions draw approximately three fourths of their people from one fourth of the population. Thus, as the requirements of society for professional manpower increases, it becomes necessary for professions to seek a wider social base from which to select recruits. Librarianship must, and should, turn for recruits to members of groups who have acquired cultural interests largely by means of education rather than from family backgrounds.

Data on the economic backgrounds of academic librarians parallel the tendencies observed in the social-origins data. The following percentages represent subjects' memories of the financial condition of their family during their childhood:

	Relatively good	Relatively poor
Major executives	43	57
Control group	50	50

Though less reliable than the data on father's occupation, this information is included because (1) it confirms the findings of the social-origins study, i.e., that seemingly unfavorable origin is no barrier to a librarian's rising to an executive post, though not necessarily to the highest-paid level, and (2) the finding that

Social, Economic, and Demographic Origins 9

subjects tend to come from high-status homes does not mean that their parents were well-to-do financially. By their testimony, the subjects appear to have come from genteel but frequently rather impecunious families.

It may well be that, in the past, librarianship has attracted people from families enjoying high status but not economic prosperity because it was a genteel profession that required less-expensive educational preparation than, say, medicine or college teaching. Better economic conditions have tended to dry up this pool of recruits, but the same forces should soon begin to supply prospective librarians from the families of laboring people who have been able to send their children to college because of the high wages labor has received since the beginning of World War II.

EDUCATIONAL LEVEL OF PARENTS

The amount of education a person has tends to correlate with his social and economic status. Caplow goes so far as to say that "the principal mechanism for the inheritance of occupational level appears to be the educational system."[7] The data to be presented in Chapter III suggest that education is also a means by which a person may overcome an unfavorable social-status heritage.

The tabulation in Table 3 shows that librarians, psychologists, and business leaders all tend to come from the families of men who are better educated than the general run of the population.[8]

TABLE 3.
LEVEL OF FATHER'S OCCUPATION
(LIBRARIANS AND OTHER GROUPS)

Occupational Group	Amount of Education	
	High School or Less	Some College or More
Academic librarians (1958)		
Major executives	63%	37%
Minor executives	58	41
Others	56	44
Psychologists (1954)	55	44
Business leaders (1952)	72	28
U.S. males 55 years and over (1940)	93	7

Although being from a family whose head lacked a college education was a handicap to those seeking either a business or professional career, it was relatively less of a disadvantage in business than it was in the professions.

As in the social-status tables, the finding is that low educational attainment on the part of one's parents is a barrier to entry into the profession but not to rising in it. The differences are somewhat smaller than those of either the social or the economic tabulations, but they are in the same direction—those from low-status backgrounds tend to rise to major executive positions more readily than those from more advantageous circumstances. That the level of education of the fathers of librarians should be higher, on the average, than that of business leaders or of the general population is not surprising. In the case of librarians, educated parents tend to pass on to their offspring not only the social status associated with education but also the regard for books and reading that teachers have fostered in them. The Committee on Recruiting Personnel of the Association of American Library Schools found that among 415 library science students who planned to enter academic librarianship, a substantial majority gave "liking for books, literature, and reading" or "liking for libraries" in response to a question about why they chose to enter this profession.[9] It is obvious that the children of high-status, well-educated parents have a better opportunity to acquire a taste for reading than do those from other types of homes. Several of the subjects of the present study whose parents had not enjoyed much formal education felt called upon to explain how they acquired their taste for books by saying, for example, that "father was self-educated...a great reader."

GEOGRAPHIC ORIGINS

Certain parts of the country offer greater inducements for people to seek professional careers than do others. Some areas are better supplied than others with the educational facilities required and have at hand many good examples of the types of institutions in which professional people work. For example, the educational poverty of large areas of the South might be expected to inhibit the development of candidates for entry into librarianship.

Table 4 indicates that this expectation is borne out in the group of librarians under study here. However, a comparison with business leaders and eminent scientists (not reproduced here) showed that, in geographic origin, the academic librarians are more nearly representative of the population as a whole than are the other two groups—groups of higher economic and social status. The tendency for the South to be deficient in the production of librarians is not so striking as is its deficient production of eminent scientists and

TABLE 4.
GEOGRAPHIC DISTRIBUTION OF SUBJECTS
AT TIME OF SURVEY (1958)

Census Region	Major Executives (231)	Minor Executives (232)	Others (244)	All Subjects (707)	U.S. Population in 1950*
Northeast	29%	36%	35%	33%	25%
North Central	31	21	23	27	29
South	21	14	27	24	30
West†	19	29	16	16	16

*U.S. Bureau of the Census, *Statistical Abstract of the United States: 1955* (76th ed.; Washington, D.C., 1955), p.16. Proportions adjusted to include British Columbia.
†Includes British Columbia and U.S. territories.

business leaders. As time goes by, the South may be increasing its capacity to produce leaders and skilled professional persons. A cross tabulation for the academic librarians by age tends to support this hypothesis: among subjects fifty years of age or older, 22 percent are from the South. Among those under fifty, the proportion is 27 percent.

It may well be that the first effects of improvement in the status of a region may be felt in the ranks of the "middle-brow" professions, of which librarianship is an example. Furthermore, during the period under study, the rate of increase in number of volumes in southern libraries has been greater than that for other parts of the country.[10] Also, its library leadership has been good.[11] The fact that an economically poor region has paid considerable attention to its libraries probably has a bearing on the apparent tendency for academic librarianship to draw relatively more recruits from the South than do other professional groups.

Considering the relative economic poverty of the region during the period covered by this study, the South is relatively well supplied with academic librarians. It is only six percentage points below par (Table 4). It was expected that the Northeast, with its great universities, would show a greater margin of superiority in number of academic librarians than it actually does. It would appear that academic library service is rather equitably distributed throughout the country on the basis of number of professional staff members available per capita of the general population.

More revealing than the simple representation of the geographic distribution of subjects during childhood is the study of their movements since then. The following tabulation illustrates this by showing in percentage the net gain or loss of each region between the time subjects were in high school and the time of the survey:

Northeast	10% gain
North Central	26% loss
South	1% gain
West	27% gain

The most dramatic feature of this tabulation is the evident tendency of the North Central region to be an exporter of library talent and of the West to import it.

The reasons for this migration pattern are not difficult to ascertain: the general westward migration of the population affects librarianship just as it does other occupations. The West must import people with all sorts of special skills and training to serve its growing population and industry. In addition to this, the wealth of various parts of the country and the willingness of governments and private institutions to spend it on academic libraries are important factors. The correlation between in-migration of academic librarians and expenditures per 1000 population on academic libraries in 1939-40 is .80. The South imported a few more librarians than its expenditures per capita would indicate, and the North Central region imported fewer than would be expected. Otherwise, generous support of academic libraries is an excellent indication that a region will need to import professional personnel. This would seem to be symptomatic of a failure on the part of the educational facilities of regions with the better-supported libraries to develop quickly enough to meet the need.

The following tabulation shows that there is a marked tendency for major executives to be more mobile geographically than the control groups. It shows the percentages of migrants in each group of subjects:

Major executives	34
Minor executives	27
Others	24

This parallels Harvey's finding that the elite among pre-World War II librarians tended to have been relatively mobile.[12] Adams and others have found this tendency among members of various professional and other elite groups.[13] The point here is that those who desired to rise in the hierarchy of academic librarianship were required to pull up stakes and move to where the opportunity lay, even if this meant moving to another region of the country, rather than to await promotion from within either a particular library or a particular geographic area.

SUMMARY

People who entered academic librarianship during the period of this study tended to come from families of rather high social and educational, but not economic, status. Lower-class origin was a barrier to entry into the profession but not to rising in it once entry was gained. Those from less-favorable social backgrounds seem to congregate in executive positions of the moderate-size institutions rather than in the highest-paid ranks of academic librarianship.

Geographically speaking, the Midwest tends to export library talent to other parts of the country while the rapidly growing West imports it. Geographic mobility is a prominent factor in the backgrounds of those who rise to executive posts. It was frequently necessary for academic librarians who desired to "get ahead" to move not only from library to library but also to move considerable distances from the places in which they were reared.

NOTES

[1] cf. Max Weber, *From Max Weber: Essays in Sociology;* trans., edited, and with an introduction by H. H. Gerth and C. Wright Mills (New York: Oxford Univ. Press, 1946), p.181.

[2] W. Lloyd Warner, Marchia Meeker, and Kenneth Eells, *Social Class in America: A Manual of Procedure for the Measurement of Social Status* (Chicago: Science Research Associates, 1949), p.140-41.

[3] Stuart Adams, "Origins of American Occupational Elites; 1900-1955," *American Journal of Sociology,* 62:360-68 (Jan. 1957).

[4] Sources: Robert R. Douglass, "The Personality of the Librarian" (Ph.D. dissertation, Univ. of Chicago, 1957, Microfilm), p.61; Stephen S. Visher, *Scientists Starred 1903-1943 in American Men of Science* (Baltimore: Johns Hopkins Univ. Press, 1947), p.533; W. Lloyd Warner, *Occupational Mobility in American Business and Industry, 1928-1952* (Minneapolis: Univ. of Minnesota Press, 1955), p.46; M'ledge Moffett, *The Social Background and Activities of Teachers' College Students* ("Teachers' College Contribution to Education," No.375 [New York: Teachers College, Columbia Univ., 1929]), p.26; Kenneth E. Clark, *America's Psychologists: A Survey of a Growing Profession* (Washington, D.C.: American Psychological Assn., 1957), p.107; Milton Wittman, *Scholarship Aid in Social Work Education* (New York: Council on Social Work Education, 1956), p.25.

[5] It is true that the dispersion of dates of birth is much greater for the librarians than for the teachers' college students.

[6] W. Lloyd Warner, Robert J. Havighurst, and Martin B. Loeb, *Who Shall Be Educated? The Challenge of Unequal Opportunities* (New York: Harper, 1944), p.100-101.

[7] Theodore Caplow, *The Sociology of Work* (Minneapolis: Univ. of Minnesota Press, 1954), p.337.

[8] Sources: Kenneth E. Clark, *America's Psychologists: A Survey of a Growing Profession* (Washington, D.C.: American Psychological Assn., 1957),

14   The Career of the Academic Librarian

p.108; W. Lloyd Warner, *Occupational Mobility in American Business and Industry, 1928-1952* (Minneapolis: Univ. of Minnesota Press, 1955), p.100.

[9] Association of American Library Schools, Committee on Recruiting Personnel, "Why Library School Students Chose the Library Profession" (n.p., 1953), p.20. (Mimeographed)

[10] Robert B. Downs, "Distribution of American Library Resources," *College and Research Libraries*, 18:236 (May 1957).

[11] For example, the authors of the two basic textbooks in academic librarianship, Louis Round Wilson *(The University Library)* and Guy R. Lyle *(The Administration of the College Library)* have both been librarians of southern universities.

[12] John F. Harvey, "Variety in the Experience of Chief Librarians," *College and Research Libraries*, 19:110 (March 1958).

[13] Stuart Adams, *op. cit.*, p.360-68; Seymour M. Lipset and Reinhard Bendix, *Social Mobility in Industrial Society* (Berkeley and Los Angeles; Univ. of California Press, 1959), p.206.

CHAPTER III

Education and Training

In 1927, Pitirim A. Sorokin described the educational system of a country as a "testing, selecting and distributing agency... a very complicated 'sieve,' which sifts 'the good' from 'the bad' future citizens, 'the able' from 'the dull,' 'those fitted for the high positions' and those 'unfitted.'"[1] More recent research, referred to in Chapter II above, has substantiated these views with detailed empirical data.

The information gathered from academic librarians shows not only that sheer amount of education is the most conspicuous factor determining who will rise to the top of the profession (the "elevator principle"), but also that the "sieve" is indeed complicated. Variations in type of college experience, as related to the librarian's subsequent career, is a fascinating topic of almost endless ramifications, some of which will be explored in the following sections.

UNDERGRADUATE EDUCATION

The subjects of this inquiry are highly educated. Only five of them (less than 1 percent of the total) lack a bachelor's degree or its equivalent.[2] For comparison, the following are the proportion of people with less than a college education in three other occupational groups:[3]

Business leaders (1952)	43%
Certified public accountants in California (1953)	27%
Professional public librarians (1948)	42%

These librarians tend to come from institutions which are larger than the average for the United States generally (see footnote to Table 5). There is a tendency for the major executives to

TABLE 5.
SIZE OF UNDERGRADUATE ALMA MATER*

(Size is in terms of the number of baccalaureate and first professional degrees granted; mean of total for years 1925 and 1935.)

Size	Major Executives (216)	Minor Executives (208)	Others (218)	Total (642)
Relatively small	56%	62%	61%	60%
Relatively large	44	38	39	40

*Information lacking for 65 subjects.
Mean size of graduating class of institutions attended by subjects: 281.
Mean size of graduating class for all institutions in United States 1935-36: 132 (U.S. Office of Education, *Biennial Survey of Education, 1934-36* [Washington, D.C., 1939], Vol. 2, Chap. IV, p.5, 48). In computing mean size of graduating class, total number of institutions (junior colleges and normal schools excluded) was the denominator, and total baccalaureate and first professional degrees the numerator. Data for 1935-36 were used because they represent the nearest available to the median date of graduation from college for the librarians studied (1931).
Proportion of subjects from institutions smaller than the mean for the United States: 26%.

have received their undergraduate training in the larger institutions more frequently than other librarians, but the difference is small and might be due to chance factors. However, tabulation of the data for size of alma mater by salary and sex brings out some significant detail (Tables 6 and 7). When major executives are compared with other subjects (Table 6), one finds that women in the top administrative positions come from large institutions more frequently

TABLE 6.
SIZE OF UNDERGRADUATE ALMA MATER—BY SEX*

	Male		Female	
Size of Institution	Major Executives (159)	Control Group (103)	Major Executives (57)	Control Group (313)
Relatively small	57%	52%	53%†	65%
Relatively large	43	48	47	35
Percentage point differences	-5		12	

*Information lacking for 75 subjects.
†Difference significant at .05 level.

than do their sisters in positions involving less responsibility. However, this is not true for the men. In the tabulation of the control group by salary and sex (Table 7), a similar situation is observed. Here both men and women who graduated from the larger

TABLE 7.
SIZE OF UNDERGRADUATE ALMA MATER RELATED TO SALARY—BY SEX*
(CONTROL GROUP ONLY)

	Male		Female	
Size of Institution	Less than $6000 (49)	$6000 or More (54)	Less than $6000 (216)	$6000 or More (97)
Relatively small	57%	48%	70%†	53%
Relatively large	43	52	30	47
Percentage point difference		9		17

*Information lacking for 60 subjects.
†Difference significant at .01 level.

colleges and universities enjoy a salary advantage, but the women benefit more than the men. Apparently a man does not need the advantage of graduation from a large school in order to attain a position of high salary or responsibility to the extent a woman does. To put it the other way, a woman may use the fact of graduation from a large institution to offset the inherent disadvantage of being a female in American society. In the language of Kendall and Lazarsfeld,[4] a relatively large alma mater may be said to be an "intervening" factor between sex and salary in librarianship, a factor which tends to mitigate somewhat the disadvantage of being a woman.

The reasons for this superiority of people who graduated from large institutions are a matter of speculation. Perhaps early acquaintance with the complexities of the curriculum and of the library of a large institution may prepare one for subsequent employment in a like institution—where most of the higher-paying jobs are to be found. A more likely guess is that the larger institutions have a national reputation whereas many of the small ones do not.

Tabulation by type of institution from which subjects received their first degrees gives the results one would expect from the foregoing analysis by size. Table 8 shows that liberal arts colleges produced more librarians than their total enrollment generally

TABLE 8.
TYPE OF UNDERGRADUATE ALMA MATER*

Type of Institution from Which First Degree Received†	Major Executives (221)	Minor Executives (219)	Others (226)	Total (666)	Total for United States (1951-52)‡
University	57%§	51%	48%	52%	54%
Liberal arts college	34∥	44	46	41	26
Teachers' college	6	3	4	5	11
Other	3	2	2	2	9

*Information lacking or foreign degree: 41 subjects. 4% of the subjects received their first degree from foreign institutions.

†Classification of institutions is according to the U.S. Office of Education, *Education Directory*, Part 3, "Higher Education, 1949-50" (Washington, D.C., 1949).

‡U.S. Office of Education, *Biennial Survey of Education, 1950-52* (Washington, D.C., 1955), Chap. IV, sec. 1, p.37. Unfortunately, this is the first year for which figures are available with universities and liberal arts colleges given separately.

§Difference between major executives and combined control group significant at .05 level.

∥Difference significant at .01 level.

would lead one to expect. They furnished 41 percent of all the academic librarians while contributing only 26 percent of the bachelor of arts degrees in the country as a whole. On the other hand, among those who aspired to a post as head of a library of any size, being from a liberal arts college was a distinct disadvantage and having one's first degree from a major university (or complex college) was an advantage. Although teachers' college graduates tend to rise in the hierarchy of the profession, it is interesting to note that this type of institution contributes less than its share of academic librarians generally. This is surprising in view of the fact that a large proportion of the subjects (35 percent) have tried teaching before coming into librarianship.

Reagan's study[5] sheds some light on the influence of liberal arts colleges in inducing students to become librarians, and on the reason graduates of this type of institution do not rise to the top as frequently as those from other types of school. Her subjects tended to credit the library facilities of the colleges and universities from which they graduated as the second-most important factor in influencing their choice of this career, but she also found that "in a few schools, however, notably a small group of liberal arts colleges, it was the most important factor." Some of her respondents credited the influence of the academic program of the liberal arts college itself as being a key factor. One said, cynically, "after taking liberal arts for four years, what can you do but become a librarian?" Others were more charitable and referred to the liberal arts program as giving students "an abiding liking for the humanities or the social services—or perhaps contrariwise a distrust of the hub-bub of a commercial or industrial life," which, in turn, made librarianship attractive.[6] Those who shrink from the hubbub of life are not likely to rise in any hierarchy, and librarianship is no exception.

Table 9 gives detailed information about the major subjects pursued by the respondents during their undergraduate days. For those who aspired to the status of major executives, a humanities background was a handicap and training in the social sciences an advantage. This finding substantiates, in part, the speculation by

TABLE 9.
MAJOR SUBJECT OF UNDERGRADUATE EDUCATION*

(Some subjects reported two or more majors;
thus, percentages total more than 100.)

Major Subject	Major Executives (226)	Minor Executives (230)	Others (236)	All (692)	Total for United States in 1942†
Humanities (including foreign languages)	64%‡	77%	78%	72%	9%
History	30	25	23	26	
Social sciences	22‡	15	14	16	9
Natural sciences	7§	12	12	10	23
Education	4	6	11	7	24
Other ∥	11	12	12	11	35

*Information lacking for 15 subjects.

†Baccalaureate and first professional degrees. Compiled from President's Commission on Higher Education, *Higher Education for American Democracy* (New York: Harper, 1947), Vol. 6, p.33.

‡Difference between major executive and combined control group significant at .01.

§ Significant at .05.

∥Library science excluded except where reported as only undergraduate major (8% of subjects). Library science degrees (.6% of the total for the United States) are so few that their inclusion or exclusion does not affect the percentage distribution in the last column.

Danton and Merritt that a student's undergraduate major might bear a "significant relationship to his success in librarianship."[7] These data also lend support to a contention of Louis R. Wilson:

> Librarianship has suffered...from the fact that the overwhelming majority of librarians have been recruited from fields in which the canons of criticism have been formulated, and in which there is a minimum of opportunity for experimentation....Consequently librarians whose background has been principally of the literary and historical character, have not been so generally concerned with the assumptions which underlie many aspects of librarianship as they might. Certainly they have not been drilled as undergraduates in the processes of hypothetical thinking and experimentation to the extent that students in the sciences and social sciences have been....[8]

(The evidence here suggests, however, that Dean Wilson's stricture is not so appropriate to history, especially where it is studied as a social science, as it is to the humanities generally.)

It is clear that graduates of technological and undergraduate professional curricula (other than librarianship) do not enter academic librarianship to any extent. Again, it will be noticed that relatively few majors in education are represented despite the tendency of librarianship to recruit one third or more of its members from among former teachers. This parallels the finding that few of the respondents are graduates of colleges of education. Academic librarianship tends to draw people trained in the liberal arts who may have tried their hands at schoolteaching, but not from among those specifically trained as educators.

Privately controlled institutions produced more than their share of the academic librarians studied: 62 percent of the subjects are from privately controlled universities and colleges, whereas this type of institution produced only 54 percent of the degrees granted in the United States for the year 1932.[9] Inasmuch as the liberal arts college is typically a private rather than a public institution,[10] the discussion above relative to liberal arts versus other types of curricula is also applicable here. Private schools frequently offer the humanistic type of education that, in turn, tends to predispose one to become a librarian rather than to enter the "hubbub of a commercial or industrial life." Also, this finding is probably related to the social-class origin of the subjects. The families of the genteel, even though economically somewhat threadbare, stratum of society from which librarians are, or have been, drawn would prefer to send their children to private rather than to public colleges if they could possibly afford it. If a generalization can be made, and all such are dangerous, librarianship tends to be more attractive to those trained in the upper-class, humanistic tradition of the private college rather than in what some regard as the pragmatic, middle-class values of the publicly supported institution exemplified by the normal school or teachers' college, and perhaps even the giant public university, of the first half of the twentieth century.

OPINIONS ABOUT UNDERGRADUATE EDUCATION

The climate of opinion among librarians in the field concerning the objectives of both general and professional education for librarianship is an important indicator of the pressures that will be brought to bear on educators. If, as Durkheim and others after him have suggested, the professions are the key to democratic life,[11] the state of opinion in a professional group is of great interest not only to the profession itself but also to society at large.

If the Williamson recommendations of 1923 represent "expert" opinion, then there is one point on which practicing librarians and experts are agreed: "as an educational preparation for library work nothing has been discovered which can take the place of a thorough college course of varied content."[12] Subjects in the present study overwhelmingly voted for an academic, as opposed to a pragmatic, emphasis in undergraduate education. Table 10 spells this out: each subject was asked to check two items from a list or to compose statements of his own. An overwhelming majority voted for emphasis on the mind-training objectives as being the most appropriate for the undergraduate preparation of future librarians. "Instrumental" aims, statements concerning training in the conduct of life, were not popular. This may reflect current dissatisfaction with so-called progressive theories of education. At any rate, adjustment to one's environment does not appear to be well regarded as a subject for higher education except in the sense that a librarian needs to feel at home in the world of ideas and to have some understanding of the larger social and economic problems of society.

That vocational preparation should also be in relatively low esteem as an undergraduate emphasis is not surprising inasmuch as most subjects chose librarianship as an occupation relatively late in their educational careers.[13] The indication is that they would not have studied library science even if it had been offered more widely as an undergraduate subject. In the free-comment sections of the questionnaire, the subjects expressed much sentiment in favor of a general academic education on the undergraduate level followed by practical training in the professional school.

TABLE 10.
OPINIONS CONCERNING THE MAIN PURPOSES
OF A COLLEGE EDUCATION*

(Subjects were asked to check the *two* items which they thought should be the most important purposes of undergraduate college education.)

Purpose	Major Executives (225)	Minor Executives (228)	Others (239)	Total (692)
Vocational preparation or pre-professional training	16†	25	27	23
Develop ability to get along with people	8	9	12	10
Develop critical faculties and appreciation for ideas	87	83	83	84
Special competence in a particular discipline	36‡	28	26	30
Understanding of community and world problems	33	36	32	34
Develop moral capacities, standards, and values	16	14	16	15
Preparation for marriage and family	0	0	1	0
Other	7	5	5	6

*Information lacking for 15 subjects.
†Significantly different from other two groups combined at .01 level.
‡.05 level.

They seem not to agree with the recommendation of the President's Commission on Higher Education that "The age-old distinction between education for living and education for making a living be discarded."[14]

In comparing the three groups of subjects, it will be seen that there is little difference in the pattern of preference of the minor executives, i.e., supervisory personnel, and that of librarians without administrative responsibilities. However, the major executives did make somewhat different choices from those of the other two groups. In general, the top administrators favored the two statements that may be characterized as academic in character more frequently than did members of the control group. On the issue of specialization, the major executives favored subject matter concentration more, and vocational preparation even less, than did the minor executives and nonexecutives.

The tendency for the major executive to espouse points of view that are broader and less utilitarian than those of the middle-managers and non-administrators is in accordance with the theory of leadership which holds that a trait essential to the true leader is that his interests be broader than that of the segment of society he leads.[15] However, there is a broad pragmatism in the position of the major administrators. Having gone through the process of mastering a special discipline enables a head librarian to understand the problems of his most highly esteemed client, the faculty member who is a productive scholar. In Danton's words:

> ... understanding of the approach, attitude of mind, and research needs of other members of the academic community cannot help but make more fruitful, easy, and effective the librarian's work with them. Lacking this understanding it is difficult for the librarian to deal with members of the faculty in terms that are wholly satisfactory to the faculty.[16]

It may well be that the head librarian feels this need more strongly than do the other members of the library staff; however, it will be noted that the statistical differences upon which this conclusion is based are relatively small.

GRADUATE EDUCATION

The most conspicuous correlate of success in academic librarianship, in so far as position or salary are measures of this, is amount of education. Table 11 shows that 81 percent of the major executives have degrees beyond the basic professional one, whereas less than one half of the control group have undergone this much training. During the period covered by this study, the doctorate in librarianship virtually, and the subject doctorate almost, assured the holder of major executive status. The master's degree in librarianship awarded as a second graduate degree (or in a few cases as the first degree, but requiring two or more years of graduate study in library science) has served as something of an entree into executive positions—minor or major. Holding a subject master's degree, however, is not much of an indicator of executive status, since more than one fourth of those without much supervisory responsibility and only a slightly greater proportion of major executives report it as the highest degree held.

24   The Career of the Academic Librarian

TABLE 11.
HIGHEST DEGREES HELD BY SUBJECTS*

Highest Degree Held	Major Executives (231)	Minor Executives (231)	Others (244)	Total (706)
Subject doctorate	14%	4%	6%	8%
Doctorate in librarianship	10	0	1	4
Subject master's	31	25	26	27
Master's in librarianship (as second graduate degree)	26	22	13	20
Subtotal: more than first professional degree	81%	51%	46%	59%
Master's in librarianship (as first professional degree)	4	9	7	7
Bachelor's in library science (as second baccalaureate degree)	10	23	31	21
Bachelor's in library science (as first baccalaureate degree)	1	6	5	4
Certificate in librarianship (or extensive training)†	1	8	8	6
Academic bachelor's only	2	4	2	3
No degrees	1	0.4	1	1

*Information lacking for one subject.
†One semester or more of formal education in librarianship.

ADVANCED SUBJECT DEGREES

In seeming contradiction to the last sentence above, Table 12, which only shows possession of a subject master's degree (as opposed to its being the highest degree held), indicates that it distinguishes major executives from other academic librarians rather well. This is a consequence of this degree's being, for many, a way station in the quest of the doctorate. Table 12 also shows that the subject master's degree confers a considerable salary advantage, particularly on the control group.

Holding a master's degree in a subject field is strongly associated with sex (Table 13), being held twice as frequently by men as by women. Thus, part of the advantage attributed to the degree may actually be due to the fact that men hold it more frequently than women, and the men have an advantage simply because they

Education and Training 25

TABLE 12.
POSSESSION OF MASTER'S DEGREE IN AN ACADEMIC SUBJECT
RELATED TO POSITION LEVEL AND SALARY*

(Proportions in this table differ from those in Table 11 because some librarians who have a subject master's also have doctorates.)

	Major Executives			Control Groups (Minor Executives and Others)		
Degrees	Less than $8000 (105)	$8000 or More (125)	Total (230)	Less than $6000 (295)	$6000 or More (167)	Total (462)
Have master's degree	42	50	46†	23†	38	28
Do not	58	50	54	77	62	72

*Information lacking for 15 subjects.
†Differences statistically significant at .01 level: total for major executives compared with total for control groups; salary level comparison for control groups.

are men. However, sex does not explain away all of the advantage enjoyed by holders of the subject master's degree. Among women, considered separately, it is an advantage to have earned this degree if one wished to become a major executive in an academic library. Here, again, it appears that securing a master's degree in a subject enables a woman to overcome the normal handicaps of her sex in the competition for advancement.

There are some interesting findings in data on the association between holding the subject master's degree and the type of library

TABLE 13.
POSSESSION OF MASTER'S DEGREE IN AN ACADEMIC SUBJECT
RELATED TO POSITION LEVEL AND SEX*

	Males			Females		
Degrees	Major Executives (169)	Control Groups (113)	Total (282)	Major Executives (62)	Control Groups (352)	Total (414)
Have master's degree	50%	44%	58%†	37%†	24%	26%
Do not	50	56	52	63	76	74

*Information lacking for 11 subjects.
†Differences significant at .01 level: totals compared with totals; female major executives with female control subjects.

work done (as opposed to salary or hierarchical position). There were only sixteen respondents with master's degrees in the natural sciences in the group. Of these only one is a major executive. However, of the fifteen in the control group, nine were earning $6000 or more a year at the time of the survey, a relatively high proportion. Holders of the master's degree in the humanities tend to concentrate in acquisitions or catalog departments of libraries. The humanities are the least, and the natural sciences the most, strongly represented among librarians engaged in branch or special collections work. This, of course, reflects a tendency for the sciences to be served by branch libraries and the humanities by the large central collection of the institution.

Most of the holders of doctorates, whether in library science or other subjects, also hold major executive posts. Among the minor executives and nonexecutives, holders of subject doctorates (in law and education included) are rare. Of the twenty-four such doctorates among the 475 respondents in the control group, nine received less than $6000 in 1958. All nine held their degrees in the humanities or social sciences (five were women; four, men). In the major executive group, the story is quite different: of the thirty-two non-library science doctorates, all but six were in the highest salary category (over $8000 per year).

Even though there may have been need for subject specialists with the doctorate in other types of library positions, the salaries and prestige of the top administrative posts won almost all of the candidates. The position of the highly educated woman, however rare she may be, is anomalous. One woman Ph.D., working in the library of a large eastern university, put it this way:

> It was my own decision to accept the small-paid Librarian's job instead of a College teaching position which I could have had with my Ph.D. I decided on it because I wanted to stay with my family in _____. In 1926, it was unthinkable that _____ would hire women professors of English. In 1958 there was a plan to admit women as undergraduates, but I have *not yet* heard of any women Faculty appointed in Liberal Arts!...I still receive much less than... inexperienced Instructors who have a Master's degree, but the mental setup here is different. These are men, and this is a man's college. And you can take it or leave it. I'm taking it.

Probably the reason academic librarianship has not capitalized on the failure of the academic disciplines to utilize female talent is that the library is, or attempts to be, part of the same social system as the teaching faculty.

TABLE 14.
TYPE OF LIBRARY SCHOOL ATTENDED
(FIRST PROFESSIONAL COURSE ONLY)*

(Classification is according to the Board of Education for Librarianship Accreditation, 1948, with new-style master's, i.e., master's awarded as first professional degree listed separately.)

Type Library School	Major Executives (211)	Minor Executives (221)	Others (227)	Total (659)
Type I†	49%‡	44%	36%	42%
Type II	25‡	29	37	30
Type III	10	8	9	9
New-style master's	7	10	11	10
Unaccredited	5	5	5	5
Foreign	-	2	1	1
Pioneer (New York State and New York Public)	4	3	1	2

*Did not graduate from a library school: 48 subjects. Proportions of nongraduates in each group: major executives, 9%; minor executives, 5%; others, 7%.

†Includes 7 subjects who have master's degrees from the University of Chicago, which, although first professional degrees, are not new-style master's degrees.

‡Difference between major executives and combined control group significant at .05 level.

Board of Education for Librarianship in 1948-49, the last year of such classification.

Table 15 shows that slightly more than half of the major executives and slightly less than half of the control subjects attended a school classified as Type I under the old Board of Education for Librarianship scheme. These findings agree with Harvey's for an earlier group of head college librarians.[20] The pre-eminence of Type I schools as suppliers of personnel for academic librarians is again seen in the ratio of subjects per one thousand graduates of each type of school: Type I, 3.2; Type II, 1.3; Type III, 1.0.

Having attended a Type I library school was some indication that a librarian would subsequently become a major executive rather than a member of the control group (Table 15), but the tendency is not as strong as anticipated. An unexpected finding is that attendance at a Type II school was something of a disadvantage to a person desiring to rise to the top of the hierarchy. It would appear that an undergraduate major in librarianship in a Type III or unac-

The situation regarding use of highly trained subject specialists in academic libraries may well change as librarianship becomes more and more complex and better-paid generally, provided that the specialists are available in the academic market place.

PROFESSIONAL EDUCATION FOR LIBRARIANSHIP

The first half of the twentieth century saw a transition from the self-made to the professionally trained academic librarian. The data in this section show some of the results of this movement.

The accreditation criteria for library schools in force when the great majority of the subjects received their training are now no longer in effect. This accrediting scheme, administered by the American Library Association's Board of Education for Librarianship, was adopted in 1933 and provided for three types of library schools.[17] Type I schools, of which there were five, were affiliated with major universities and offered a first professional degree or certificate for one post-baccalaureate year and a master's degree for a second year. Some Type I schools also offered the doctorate but only the University of Chicago awarded any before 1951. Type II schools, sixteen in number, offered a first professional degree for one year of graduate work but nothing further. Most of these were attached to universities, but five were affiliated with technical institutes, vocational schools, or women's colleges. Type III schools (there were thirteen of these in 1949) offered one year of library training as part of an undergraduate curriculum. These schools tended to emphasize preparation of students for positions in school libraries.[18]

In addition to the schools accredited by the Board of Education for Librarianship, a number of colleges offered majors in librarianship, some of which were accredited by other agencies. There were also two early schools in New York that have been designated here as the "pioneer" library schools.

Following World War II, a new pattern of library education began to emerge. In 1948 the first "new style" degree was awarded.[19] This new degree, a master's given as the first professional degree in librarianship, is now the prevailing degree, but only 10 percent of the respondents to this study have it. It will be noted in Table 14 that holders of this new-style master's degree are tending to rise in the profession rather frequently, considering the brief period it has been offered. Nevertheless, inasmuch as the total impact of the new-style master's degree was small during the period of this survey, holders of this degree have not been listed separately in any of the tabulations except Table 14. They are simply included with other alumni of a school as classified by the credited school gave as good or better preparation for an administrative post as a graduate program of limited scope represented by the Type II schools.

TABLE 15.
TYPE OF LIBRARY SCHOOL ATTENDED RELATED TO SALARY IN 1958*

| | Major Executives ||| Control Groups |||
Type of Library School†	Less than $8000 (101)	$8000 or More (110)	Total (211)	Less than $6000 (279)	$6000 or More (164)	Total (443)
Type I	45%‡	59%	53%‡	37%§	59%	45%
Type II	32	22	27§	42§	29	37
Type III	13	11	12	11§	5	9
Other	10	8	9	10	7	9
Percentage of total subjects with no library school training	5	12	8	7	4	6
Total subjects	(106)	(125)	(231)	(299)	(171)	(470)

*Information lacking for six subjects.
†Holders of the new-style master's degree are not separated but are included in the totals for the school attended under the classification it had before inaugurating the new program.
‡Difference between groups significant at .05 level.
§Difference significant at .01 level.

Some speculation on the reasons for the relatively poor showing[21] of Type II school graduates in ascending the hierarchical ladder would seem to be in order. According to the Williamson theory,[22] the schools offering a year of study in library science on the graduate level (i.e., Type II schools) should have a better record than those offering it on the undergraduate level (Type III schools), but in so far as the subjects here are concerned, this is not the case. Two possible explanations might be: (1) Since relatively few graduates of Type III and unclassified curricula enter academic librarianship, having been trained in this type of school may be said to represent a barrier to entry into this, as opposed to other, branches of the profession. Just as in the case of other barriers to entry (e.g., low social-class origin), the energy that enables a person to break into the profession despite this handicap

30   The Career of the Academic Librarian

also enables him to rise in it. (2) The Type III curriculum places a premium on early choice of librarianship as a career, whereas placing all library science work on the graduate level tends to attract what one respondent called "semi-failures" from other fields. Data showing the advantages of recruiting people for the profession during their college days will be presented in Chapter IV. Suffice it to say here that, although the Type III curricula do not represent the ideal way of doing this, they did succeed in attracting promising young people into academic librarianship.

It will be noted that relatively more major executives than others lack library school training altogether. For the most part, these are scholars who have entered librarianship at the top from faculty positions in colleges and universities. Either this practice is decreasing or there is a tendency for such appointments to be made late in the life of the appointee. Of the nineteen subjects in the major executive group with no formal library school training, thirteen were fifty or more years old in 1958. It would appear that the professionally trained librarian is taking over the last stronghold of scholar-turned-librarian, the position of chief executive. The fact that scholars in other fields can now find employment in their own discipline more readily than in the depression years may account in part for this tendency, along with, of course, the advantages afforded by professional training.

Table 16, which shows the results of a sort of popularity contest to determine the relative prestige of library schools among

TABLE 16.
REPUTATION OF VARIOUS LIBRARY SCHOOLS*

(Subjects were asked to name the three schools which seem to produce the greatest number of outstanding librarians.)

| Name of library school | Percentages of Subjects Voting for Each School ||||
	Major Executives (176)	Minor Executives (175)	Others (149)	Total (500)
Columbia	74%	82%	84%	80%
Chicago	75	62	50	63
Illinois	62	53	52	56
Michigan	41	42	34	40
California	11	14	21	15
Other	13	22	25	21

*207 subjects (29%) did not respond to this question; 20 (3%) named more than three schools and were excluded from tabulation.

the respondents, demonstrates the proposition that the profession is aware of the larger staffs, better financial condition, and richer curricula of the Type I schools.[23] Each of the five Type I schools received more votes than any representative of the other types.

The factors producing this favorable image of the Type I schools in the minds of the subjects are various: the very fact of having enjoyed this prestige classification is one factor; another is the tendency for the many Type I graduates to vote for their own school out of loyalty. However, the fact that Type I schools more frequently made special provision or had special courses for prospective college and university librarians than did other types is certainly involved.[24]

The influence of the specialized curriculum of the University of Chicago, which concentrated on advanced rather than first-professional work, is evident in Table 16. Its popularity declines as one goes down the levels of the hierarchy. This tendency is also seen in the ratings of Illinois and, to some extent, those of Michigan but not in the ratings of Columbia or of California. Apparently the curricula of the latter two schools, before 1953, at least, appealed more to "working" librarians than to major executives. In the same vein, the program of schools other than Type I have more appeal to minor executives and nonexecutives than to the top executives. The subjects tend to admire the type of school from which they received their own training or which emphasize the kind of training that is useful in the level of work they are doing or supervising. There is, perhaps, some support here for the often recommended policy of formally recognizing two or perhaps three levels of librarianship.[25] The present American Library Association policy of accrediting only schools offering the master's as a first library degree will certainly tend to reduce this differentiation when the need may be to have it accentuated.[26]

The reputation of the Graduate Library School of the University of Chicago cannot be explained on the basis of the number of graduates it has produced. One obvious explanation is found in the fact that it had a virtual monopoly on awarding the doctorate in librarianship until relatively recently. However, an analysis of subjects who hold its first professional degree indicates that they have done well also: fifteen out of seventeen were earning more than $6000 a year in 1958. Thus, it would appear that the reputation of this school in the minds of academic librarians is in accordance with reality. Even though this was not the primary aim of the Graduate Library School, the "scholarly" approach to library education which it emphasizes has had the pragmatic result of producing library administrators and other leaders of "practical" librarianship. From the first, the intention of the Graduate Library School has been to stress the "cultural, literary, bibliographical and social aspects of librarianship as a learned profession."[27] Perhaps its success was due in large measure to the work of Louis R. Wilson, Dean from 1932-40.

Dean Wilson possessed both broad scholarly interests and highly successful experience as a library administrator. Before his appointment there had been "scepticism and lack of understanding among many librarians" to whom "the courses, projects, and philosophy of the school seemed...a bit long-haired and impractical."[28] One means by which acceptance was fostered was through a series of summer institutes, workshops, and conferences for the rank and file of the profession which the Graduate Library School sponsored.[29] Evidence for the great need of more such in-service education for academic librarians will be presented in subsequent chapters.

As will be seen in the next section, not all librarians are enthusiastic about the theoretical approach to education for librarianship represented by the Chicago program. Many feel that it has resulted in neglect of the arts and techniques of the profession. Thus, the popularity of some of the other Type I schools may rest on a basis quite different from that of Chicago. As one respondent put it:

> At Columbia the idea was expressed that cataloging and the techniques should be taught on the job anyway and not as part of professional college work. After the old hands who had this special training at Illinois and California die off who is to teach these young upstarts?

What the respondent attributes to the School of Library Service at Columbia University was to be seen par excellence at Chicago.

In contradiction to the opinion given above, other librarians feel that the Chicago approach is in the end more truly pragmatic than a preoccupation with technical detail. As one respondent, a branch librarian in education, phrased it:

> Students in library school continuously complain that there is too much "busy work" and repetition of subject matter in assigned readings.... If less emphasis was placed on the routine tasks and more on the importance of the work and the challenge it would add to the number going into the profession.... The rewards of the profession are well worth the effort of the library education courses but one does not know this when struggling for an obscure fact or proper spacing on a catalog card.

The evidence in this section would seem to support this view.

ADVANCED DEGREES IN LIBRARY SCIENCE

During the professional lives of the subjects represented here, the structure of advanced education for librarianship changed radically. The once influential master's degree in librarianship given for a second postgraduate year was virtually abandoned in favor of the new-style, one-year master's program by the operation of a sort of educational Gresham's law. Increased production of professional doctorates did not completely fill the gap left by the demise of the old-style master's degree.

The passing of the old-style master's degree has probably affected women more than men in the profession. In the first place, it was primarily a feminine degree (see Table 17). Furthermore, possession of this degree was of great advantage to the woman who aspired to becoming a head librarian: almost half of the female major executives have it as compared to one quarter of the men in that category.

TABLE 17.
POSSESSION OF OLD-STYLE MASTER'S DEGREE IN
LIBRARY SCIENCE RELATED TO SEX

(Old-style master's degree means the master's degree given for two or more post-baccalaureate years, as second professional degree.)

Degrees	Major Executives			Control Groups		
	Male (169)	Female (62)	Total (231)	Male (113)	Female (351)	Total (464)
Have old-style master's	25%*	47%	31%*	16%	21%	20%
Do not have	75	53	69	84	79	80

*Difference significant at .01 level: male with female major executives; total major executives with total for control group.

The situation is similar when salary, rather than hierarchical status, is considered as the criterion of "success." Table 18 shows that holding an old-style master's degree is of considerably more salary advantage to a woman than to a man. In other words, here is another case in which an educational factor is shown to mitigate the salary disadvantage associated with being a woman.

Thus, from the feminine point of view, there is a melancholy aspect to the discontinuance of the second-year master's degree programs: unless doctoral study becomes more popular among women than it is now, or unless some other substitute is found, the closing of this pathway to top level positions may further widen the

TABLE 18.
SALARY RELATED TO POSSESSION OF OLD-STYLE
MASTER'S DEGREE BY SEX
(CONTROL GROUPS ONLY)*

	Totals		Possess Old-Style Master's		Do Not Have Old-Style Master's	
Salary	Male (113)	Female (351)	Male (18)	Female (75)	Male (95)	Female (276)
Less than $6000	46%†	70%	39%	53%	47%†	74%
$6000 or More	54	30	61	47	53	26
Percentage point differences	24		14		27	

*Information lacking for 12 subjects.
†Differences (male and female) significant at .01.

gap between men and women in opportunity for rising in the academic library profession.

Of the twenty-five holders of the doctorate in librarianship among the respondents, only three were women. Also disproportionate is the number who received their degrees from the University of Chicago, all but six. The postwar expansion of doctoral programs in institutions other than Chicago had only begun to have effect on the group covered by this study.

As Danton has shown for the whole corpus of holders of doctoral degrees in librarianship, librarians with this degree tend to gravitate to the highest administrative positions in academic libraries.[30] Of the holders of doctorates in library science in the present group, all but two are major executives and all but six are in the top salary category ($8000 or more a year in 1958).

If, as has been suggested above, the chief librarian without formal library training is disappearing from the scene, the highly trained professional is in the process of arriving to take his place. It will be recalled that of the nineteen subjects in the major executive group without library training, thirteen were fifty or more years of age in 1958. In contrast to this, of the twenty-three holders of doctorates in library science in similar positions, only seven were fifty years old or older in 1958. Their mean age was 46.6 years. This is not surprising inasmuch as the first library science doctorate was not awarded until 1930; as of 1959, "more than 41 percent of the total" was produced in the past six years," i.e., 1953-59.[31]

In addition to those who actually hold library science doctorates, twenty major and two minor executives report having work in progress toward one. It would appear that having started work on the degree serves the person who aspires to a top executive post almost as well as having attained it. This is yet another reason to add to those advanced by Danton to explain the low ratio between the total number of degrees actually granted and the number of students who embark on doctoral programs in librarianship.[32]

In the group surveyed, the doctorate in librarianship is even rarer than the subject doctorate (see Table 11). As advanced programs in library science expand and spread to more institutions,[33] it remains to be seen whether the doctor's degree will continue to represent a golden key to a highly paid executive post. On the other hand, with the discontinuance of the second-year master's programs and the absorption of nearly all available holders of subject doctorates in regular teaching assignments, there is a considerable gap to be filled if level of education is to continue to be a major criterion in the selection of library executives.

OPINIONS CONCERNING EDUCATION FOR LIBRARIANSHIP

Although there is evidence that they are already aware of this,[34] leaders of the profession may be further disheartened to see the strength of the demand from the field for a utilitarian emphasis in library science education. The fourth item of Table 19 shows "Practical help in technique" to be the most popular objective of library education in the opinion of all three groups of respondents. However, further examination of the data indicates that this does not necessarily mean that academic librarians are an anti-intellectual lot.

Ever since Charles C. Williamson first strongly recommended it in 1923,[35] report after report and survey after survey have urged that library schools emphasize the scholarly, as opposed to the technical, aspects of the curriculum, especially in the training of academic librarians. For example, the College and University Postwar Planning Committee of the American Library Association recommended "that the library schools continue and accelerate the trend toward introducing more intellectual content into the curriculum."[36] Table 19 shows that the subjects do not entirely endorse this recommendation. By far the most popular statement of objectives for library school education was "practical help in techniques." Since each subject had four votes, this does not mean that everyone voting for this aspect thought it the most important, but it does mean that few were willing that training in technique be given

TABLE 19.
OPINIONS CONCERNING OBJECTIVES OF INSTRUCTION
IN LIBRARY SCIENCE

(Subjects were asked to indicate the four items which in their opinions are the most important things a student preparing for academic librarianship might get out of library science courses.*)

Objective	Major Executives (227)	Minor Executives (230)	Others (240)	Total (697)
Knowledge of library organization	59%	54%	54%	55%
Knowledge of origin and development of academic libraries	20†	7	5	11
Appreciation for library's place in higher education	63‡	58	51	57
Practical help in technique	75†	89	92	85
Problems of one special type of institution	11	13	13	12
General acquaintance with titles in broad areas§	65‡	73	72	70
Attitudes of accuracy, system, and speed	31	33	35	33
Knowledge of ways of evaluating library use	42	38	42	40
Knowledge of history of language, books, and printing	21	24	22	22
Other	7	4	6	6

*10 subjects did not respond to this item on the questionnaire.
†Significant at .01 level.
‡Difference between this group and the other two combined significant at .05 level.
§ Full statement of this objective read: "General acquaintance with important titles in each of the broad curricular fields—social science, humanities, science technology." For full statements of the other items, see copy of questionnaire in Appendix I.

a minor role in education for librarianship. To balance this popularity accorded to technique, it should be noted that the statement which came in second, "acquaintance with titles in broad areas," does involve the intellectual content of the curriculum.

The issue is not simply one of pragmatic versus scholarly content: the subjects want a great many things emphasized in the first-year curriculum. The problem is similar to the perennial one of the architect: people want a two-story house with all the rooms on the first floor. A blend of utility and theory is desired, more of each than can be fitted into a single year's course. Although perhaps the old-style master's programs were sometimes merely more-of-the-same appendages to the first-year curriculum, their influence, demonstrated by the data present earlier in this chapter, indicates that there is a real need for distinct levels of training. However, this is not to say that technique should be relegated to one level and theory to another, but rather that there should be a balance between technique and theory, between general and special education for librarianship on all levels. General and special education should go on side by side, or better, be intertwined with one another so that technique is taught in terms of principles rather than skills. As the President's Commission on Higher Education has pointed out, "professional schools defeat their own purposes when they allow technical and special courses to crowd general education from their curriculums."[37] This conclusion is supported by many studies not only in librarianship, but also of education for other professions, the most recent example being seen in two studies of the programs of schools of business administration, both of which called for more theory and less how-to-do-it content.[38]

The two items relating to the history of libraries, language, books, and printing were distinctly unpopular among the respondents. The Public Library Inquiry made a similar finding.[39] This may well indicate that there should be more rather than less emphasis on the historical roots of librarianship. Or perhaps a different approach to these topics is needed. The overwhelming demand for an emphasis on techniques may stem from lack of appreciation for the ends, as opposed to the means, of librarianship, and these are to be found by studying bibliography in historical perspective.

Just as in the case of opinion regarding the objectives of undergraduate education, there is a marked tendency for the major executives to take a somewhat broader view than others of the objectives of library education. The item on technique is considerably less popular among them than it is among members of the other two groups. On the other hand, general bibliographic knowledge seems to be of relatively less interest to major executives than to others. Utility may be again raising its head: acquaintance with bibliography is of more immediate use to those engaged in reference, public service, and technical processes work than it is to head librarians. But, in general, library executives follow the principle that leaders must take a broader view of affairs than their subordinates.[40]

The evidence here does not suggest an answer to those who complain that the curricula of present-day library schools are excessively heterogeneous.[41] There is no clear consensus among practicing librarians about what the objectives of such training should be. This is in contrast to the definite consensus that undergraduate education should be broadly academic in character. The problem of library school emphasis is much more controversial. From the remarks made by subjects in response to free-comment sections of the questionnaire, there is a definite need for a new synthesis in education for librarianship, but there is no agreement about what it should be.

Even among those who demand a great deal of emphasis on technique in education for librarianship, some realize that the apparent failure of new librarians to deal with technique does not result from a simple failure on the part of many library schools to teach necessary skills. One head catalog librarian, who checked statements referring to technique in the formal section of the questionnaire, touched on most of the key issues in her comments on the problem, including what is perhaps the crucial one, selection of students:

> I should like to see a higher scholarly and intellectual quality in the librarian trained and recommended for academic work. There seems to be too little selectivity in the library schools in recommendations for academic positions. In short, I have had to work with people who came quite well recommended who were simply not bright enough to do more than a barely adequate job in cataloging in a first rank college.
>
> More emphasis on wide general education, plenty of languages, etc. De-emphasize specialized training for the young beginner. Let the library school send out a person well prepared with necessary skills and who has served her apprenticeship, as she must no matter how specialized her training. Then she is better prepared to decide on her specialty when she has also decided to stick to librarianship as a career. I think the old undergraduate program such as Simmons College offered is highly suitable for many librarians and many positions and an excellent base on which to establish further study toward an administrative career. It seems to be that many librarians are being over-trained and badly trained for the jobs they are to do.

This librarian's habit of referring to all librarians as "she" foreshadows further discussion of that topic in the chapters to follow. Similarly, her reference to "apprenticeship," i.e., to a role of experience, is an indication of discussion to come.

SUMMARY

Undergraduate Education. Graduates of the larger, more complex colleges and universities enjoy an advantage in securing positions of administrative responsibility and/or high salary. This is particularly true of women. Majors in the social sciences fare better than those in the humanities in securing executive posts. The great majority of academic librarians feel that it is most important that undergraduate education develop the critical faculties of future librarians and enhance their appreciation for ideas. People in positions calling for leadership, even more than others, tend to favor a general-academic, rather than a preprofessional or social-adjustment, emphasis in undergraduate education.

Graduate Education (Non-Library Science). Having earned a subject master's degree tends to confer a salary advantage on the ordinary librarian; but, unless the candidate also has a doctorate, this degree seems to have had little influence on the selection of major executives. The subject master's degree is held more frequently by men than by women librarians, but it is of more advantage to the latter, i.e., holding a master's degree helps a woman overcome the disadvantage of being a female in the male society of the academic community. Although there may well be a need for persons with subject doctorates in middle-management and nonexecutive posts, most of the available supply has been absorbed in the chief executive category.

Library Science Education. Type of library school attended by subjects is related to the attainment of executive rank, but it is even more strongly associated with salary. First-year graduates of schools with faculties recruited to support advanced, as well as basic, programs enjoy a competitive advantage in securing high-level posts. Graduation from an undergraduate library science program is a barrier to entry into academic librarianship, but people with the qualities that enable them to overcome this barrier frequently rise in the profession.

The second-year master's degree in library science was an influential degree, particularly among women. Doctorates in library science were not plentiful during the period covered by this study, but the practice of appointing people with this degree to executive positions seems to be supplanting the older tendency to recruit executives from among members of the faculty who have subject doctorates but not library science training.

Opinion is strongly divided on the question of whether library education should be "theoretical" or "practical." Working academic librarians tend to favor the latter emphasis. Evidence here supports the suggestion that different levels of training for different levels of work in libraries might resolve this dilemma.

NOTES

[1] Pitirim A. Sorokin, *Social Mobility* (New York: Harper, 1927), p.188.

[2] If no "equivalents" (e.g., certificates from library schools not connected with educational institutions) are included, the number is twenty-one and the proportions 3 percent.

[3] W. Lloyd Warner and James C. Abegglen, *Big Business Leaders in America* (New York: Harper, 1955), p.47; A. B. Carson, *The Public Accounting Profession in California* (Los Angeles: Univ. of California, 1958), p.212; Alice I. Bryan, *The Public Librarian: A Report of the Public Library Inquiry* (New York: Columbia Univ. Press, 1952), p.57.

[4] Patricia L. Kendall and Paul F. Lazarsfeld, "Problems of Survey Analysis" in Robert K. Merton and Paul F. Lazarsfeld, eds., *Continuities in Social Research* (Glencoe, Ill.: Free Press, 1950), p.157.

[5] Agnes L. Reagan, *A Study of Factors Influencing College Students To Become Librarians* ("ACRL Monograph," No.21 [Chicago: Assn. of College and Research Libraries, American Library Assn., 1958]), p.71.

[6] *Ibid.*

[7] J. Periam Danton and LeRoy C. Merritt, "Characteristics of the Graduates of the University of California School of Librarianship" (Univ. of Illinois Library School, "Occasional Papers," No.22, June 1951. Mimeographed), p.16.

[8] Louis R. Wilson, "The Objectives of the Graduate Library School in Extending the Frontiers of Librarianship," in *New Frontiers in Librarianship* (Chicago: Graduate Library School, Univ. of Chicago, 1940), p.21.

[9] U.S. President's Commission on Higher Education, *Higher Education for American Democracy* (New York: Harper, 1947), Vol. 6, p.34-35. Other years show similar proportions.

[10] Richard H. Ostheimer: *A Statistical Analysis of the Organization of Higher Education in the United States, 1948-1949* (New York: Columbia Univ. Press, 1951), p.85.

[11] Emile Durkheim, *On the Division of Labor in Society:* [trans.] by George Simpson (New York: Macmillan, 1933), p.4, 159 ff. See also Theodore Caplow, *The Sociology of Work* (Minneapolis: Univ. of Minnesota Press, 1954), p.102.

[12] Charles C. Williamson, *Training for Library Service: A Report Prepared for the Carnegie Corporation of New York* (New York, 1923), p.28.

[13] Evidence for this statement is presented in Chapter IV.

[14] U.S. President's Commission on Higher Education, *op. cit.*, p.61.

[15] Philip Selznick, *Leadership in Administration* (Evanston, Ill.: Row, Peterson, 1957), p.143.

[16] J. Periam Danton, "Doctoral Study in Librarianship in the United States," *College and Research Libraries*, 20:449 (Nov. 1959).

[17] For an extended discussion of education for librarianship, consult Robert D. Leigh, "The Education of Librarians," Part IV of Alice I. Bryan, *op. cit.*, p.229-425.

[18] *Ibid.*, p.310-12.

[19] American Library Association. Board of Education for Librarianship, "The Librarian [Report for 1947-48]," *ALA Bulletin*, 42:445 (Oct. 15, 1948).

[20] John F. Harvey, *The Librarian's Career: A Study of Mobility* ("ACRL Microcard Series," No.85 [Rochester, N.Y.: Univ. of Rochester Press, 1957]), p.25.

[21] Following are the data for graduates of library schools with those from Type I schools excluded:

	Major Executives (100)	Control Group (234)
Type II	56%	70%
Type III and unaccredited	44	30

[22] Charles C. Williamson, *op. cit.*, p.5-6 ff.

[23] Leigh in Alice I. Bryan, *op. cit.*, p.338, 343, 408 *et passim*.

[24] *Ibid.*, p.343.

[25] For a discussion of two or three level library education, see J. Periam Danton, *Education for Librarianship: Criticisms, Dilemmas, and Proposals* (New York: School of Library Service, Columbia Univ., 1946), p.24-26.

[26] American Library Association, Board of Education for Librarianship, "Standards for Accreditation," *ALA Bulletin*, 46:48-49 (Feb. 1952). However, consideration is being given to the problem: cf. David K. Berninghausen, ed., "Undergraduate Library Education: Standards, Accreditation, Articulation" (Minneapolis: Institute on Undergraduate Library Education, Univ. of Minnesota, 1959); and American Library Association, Committee on Accreditation, "Standards and Guide for Undergraduate Library Science Programs," *ALA Bulletin*, 52:695-700 (Oct. 1958).

[27] Statement (1923) of the Chicago Library Club asking for the establishment of such a school, quoted in Joseph L. Wheeler, *Progress and Problems in Education for Librarianship* (New York: Carnegie Corporation of New York, 1946), p.74.

[28] *Ibid.*, p.75

[29] Harriet E. Howe, "Two Decades in Education for Librarianship," *Library Quarterly*, 12:569 (July 1942).

[30] J. Periam Danton, "Doctoral Study in Librarianship in the United States," *College and Research Libraries*, 20:449 (Nov. 1959).

[31] *Ibid.*, p.436-38

[32] *Ibid.*, p.443

[33] *Ibid.*, p.449. Nearly one quarter of the 129 holders of doctorates in 1959 received their degrees in 1957, 1958, or 1959.

[34] *Ibid.*, p.440-41.

[35] Charles C. Williamson, *Training for Library Service* (New York, 1923).

[36] American Library Association. Association of College and Research Libraries. College and University Postwar Planning Committee, *College and University Libraries and Librarianship* (Chicago: A.L.A., 1946), p.87.

[37] U.S. President's Commission on Higher Education, *op. cit.*, p.82.

[38] Frank C. Pierson, *The Education of American Businessmen* (New York:

McGraw-Hill, 1959); Robert A. Gordon and James E. Howell, *Higher Education for Business* (New York: Columbia Univ. Press, 1959).

[39] Alice I. Bryan, *op. cit.*, p.70.

[40] Philip Selznick, *loc. cit.*

[41] Betty Bacon, "My Year in Library School—Some Second Thoughts," *Library Journal*, 84:1741-44 (June 1, 1959).

CHAPTER IV

Career Factors

This chapter will consider the ways in which academic librarians have come into the profession, some of the things they have been doing since entering, and the manner in which they react to their experience. The objective is to throw light on the influence these factors have on the role a librarian plays on the stage of his profession.

DECISION TO BECOME A LIBRARIAN

Previous studies have shown that, for many librarians, this occupation was not the first vocational choice.[1] The academic librarians in this study exhibit the same tendency. Over 60 percent waited until after college before finally deciding to become librarians.

Although academic librarians typically delay making a final commitment to this vocational choice until after their college years, Table 20 indicates that more than half of them entertained the idea before or during college. For many, then, the idea of becoming a librarian was something one considered and then stored away while he tried something else. However, it will be noted that psychologists (Table 20) tend to consider entering that profession even later. This is probably due to the visibility factor—in general, children have more contacts with librarians than with psychologists. However, they have much more opportunity to observe the teaching profession than either librarianship or psychology. Thus, future teachers typically decide to enter teaching early in life.[2] For example, Stewart found that 66 percent of a group of experienced teachers recalled that they had finally made up their minds to enter teaching by the time they enrolled in college.[3] The corresponding proportion for

TABLE 20.
TIME OF FIRST CONSIDERATION OF LIBRARIANSHIP AS A CAREER
(AS RECALLED BY SUBJECTS)*

	Males				Females		
Time of First Consideration	Major Executives (205)	Control Group (396)	Major Executives (152)	Control Group (105)	Major Executives (53)	Control Group (294)	Psychologists[†]
Before college	16%‡	24%	11%	11%	32%	29%	5%
During college	50§	36	53	34	42	37	50
After college	34	40	37	55	26	34	43

*Information lacking for 26 major executives and 80 control subjects.
†Kenneth E. Clark, *America's Psychologists* (Washington, D.C.: American Psychological Assn., 1957), p.109. No response, 2%.
‡Significant at .05 level.
§Differences significant at .01 level.

academic librarians is 11 percent. Bauer expresses the principle of visibility as a factor in vocational choice with an interesting twist:

> ...librarianship is not a uniformed occupation. Almost all children are captivated by a uniform. Firemen and policemen are, of course, identified by their uniform or the badges of their offices: the revolver and night stick. The doctor is distinguished by a white coat and stethoscope or by that mysterious badge of his calling—the little black bag. ...
> Many boys, particularly farm boys, never use a library until they reach high school. ...Youth cannot dream of what youth has not experienced.[4]

It has been further suggested that, in a sense, the unflattering stereotype of the librarian as a "single, middle-age woman with shell-rim glasses, ground gripper shoes, etc., etc." is a "uniform."[5] This unfavorable image, although it may not fit the "typical" librarian at all, is a factor in making the profession "visible," but in an unflattering light.

Some rather high-status occupations tend to win their converts rather late in life. College teaching is one of these. In a Minnesota study, only 37 percent of the subjects had seriously considered college teaching while still undergraduates, and very few said that they had begun to think of this possibility before entering college.[6] Lack of early contact is a factor here and so is the social distance between the professor and the undergraduate student. This social distance factor may also be partly responsible for preventing early selection of academic librarianship as a career.

Typically, men are later than women in considering librarianship as a career and in making their final decision. Both Douglass and Bryan found this to be true for their groups,[7] and Tables 20 and 21 indicate that it holds for academic librarians also. Douglass logically attributes some of this difference to the fact that the lives of many men are interrupted by a period of military service. Early consideration of the possibility of librarianship as a career appears to be more strongly and consistently related to subsequent attainment of a high position in the library hierarchy than does an early final decision. However, among males (Table 21), early decision is definitely associated with a future role as a major executive and would be even more strongly so if those who enter major-executive status directly from faculty positions were excluded from the tabulation.

TABLE 21.
TIME OF FINAL CHOICE OF LIBRARIANSHIP AS A CAREER*

			Males		Females	
Time of Decision	Major Executives (229)	Control Group (453)	Major Executives (167)	Control Group (112)	Major Executives (62)	Control Group (341)
Before college	7%	10%	3%	1%	18%	13%
During college	30	27	31	25	29	28
After college	63	63	66†	74	53	59

*Information lacking for 2 major executives and 23 control subjects.
†Significant difference at .05 level.

Age at which one obtained his first full-time position in a library (Table 22) further illuminates the question of late-versus-early commitment to library work. Here, again, men are typically older than women, and youth at entry is, to a degree, associated with future status as an executive. However, the largest gap is between the minor executives and the nonexecutives.

Contrary to the finding from the data on the time of decision to enter the profession, actual age at entry into a full-time library

TABLE 22.
AGE AT ENTERING LIBRARIANSHIP*

	Male			Female		
Age at Entrance	Major Executives (166)	Minor Executives (65)	Others (47)	Major Executives (62)	Minor Executives (162)	Others (190)
Mean age of entry†	27.1	27.8	29.2	24.3	24.6	27.9‡
Standard deviation in years	6.4	6.2	7.0	4.9	5.1	7.3
Interquartile range	23-30	24-31	24-32	21-27	21-25	22-41

*Information lacking for 15 subjects.
†Age in years at time of obtaining first full-time position in a library.
‡Difference between female executives (major and minor combined) and female nonexecutives meets a T-test at .001 level of significance. (T-test is a standard means of evaluating the statistical significance of the difference between two means.)

position is a stronger indication of future executive status among women than among men. This may reflect a stronger influence of a preprofessional job in library work among female executives than among males. Some of the data about influences on decision point to this conclusion: Female major executives tend to credit clerical or substitute work in a library as influencing their decision to enter the field permanently more frequently than do males.

The ages of nonexecutives at the time of obtaining the first full-time position vary more than those of executives. The large standard deviation and interquartile ranges in age among the nonexecutives is due to the heavy concentration of late entrants in this group—a quarter of the nonexecutives entered library work after age forty. This is interesting in view of the finding of Danton and Merritt that "students 35 years of age and over, if discriminately selected, will do at least as well academically in library school as those less than 35 years old."[8] These two findings are not incompatible. Carefully selected older entrants may be just as competent as the younger ones, but they simply do not have time to gain executive positions before they reach an age at which administrations arbitrarily cease to consider people for promotion to positions of responsibility.

If the United States continues to be a "nation of youth worshippers"[9] in the future as it has been in the past, older candidates who are strongly motivated will continue to present a counseling problem to library school admissions officers. If the candidate is a woman over forty with an insatiable desire to become an executive, the counselor has a grave dilemma to face. In the group studied here, none of the female major executives entered the profession after age forty, only one of the female minor executives did, but thirteen of the nonexecutives were over this age at the time they accepted their first full-time library position.

MOTIVATION FOR ENTERING LIBRARIANSHIP

In advising potential recruits to academic librarianship, a counselor might well wish to consider whether or not experience with libraries has been instrumental in persuading a particular person to consider this line of work. In the first place, the finding here agrees with that of Reagan,[10] about one third of the subjects volunteered the information that experience with libraries had been influential in their decision to join the profession. Furthermore, among academic librarians, this factor is mentioned more frequently as the position of the respondents in the hierarchy of the profession increases. Proportions of the three hierarchical groups crediting previous experience with libraries as influencing their decision to become librarians are: major executives, 36 percent; minor executives, 29 percent; others, 27 percent.

To carry the question a step further, our hypothetical counselor might wish to know whether type of contact with libraries seems to have a bearing on the future career of the beginning librarian. Table 23 indicates that this factor might be worth considering. These percentages represent a breakdown of the total number of respondents who mentioned contact with libraries as a factor influencing them to choose this occupation:

TABLE 23.
CONTACTS WITH LIBRARIES REPORTED AS INFLUENCING CHOICE OF LIBRARIANSHIP AS A CAREER

Type of Contact	Major Executive	Control Group
Student assistant	58%	50%
Clerical work	19	31
Patron	12	11
Faculty member	8	1
Orientation or other instruction in library use	2	8

The tabulation shows that service as a student assistant is the strongest indicator of future major-executive status. Experience with clerical work in a library is a contraindication, probably because it tends to be a feminine attribute. Instruction in the use of libraries, however important it might have been in other respects, seems to have been a minor influence in attracting students to librarianship. Furthermore, those who rose to chief executive status very seldom recall such instruction's having influenced them to enter the profession.

Now that what influenced a person to enter librarianship has been asked, the next question is obviously, "Who?" The data here support Reagan's finding that librarians generally attribute the influence of individuals, particularly other librarians, as being a major factor in their decision to embark on this career.[11] A tabulation, not reproduced here, shows that academic librarians are probably in the best position to select and encourage the most promising candidates for the profession. This is particularly true for men. Proportionally more male major executives report having been influenced by college and university librarians than do either females of like status or members of the control group of either sex. Considering only the minor and nonexecutives and accepting salary as the criterion of "success," there is a correlation between recalling the influence of a college or university librarian and the salary status of the subject. Again, this correlation is much stronger for men than for women.

These facts lead to an interesting speculation: Academic librarians are well aware that opportunities for rising in the profession are greater for men than for women. Therefore, it may well be that, in advising potential candidates for the professions, academic librarians tend to discourage women who have strong ambitions for advancement.[12] In a way, this advice may be "good"; however, it has the effect of robbing the profession of aggressive female talent.[13]

Moreover, the sex composition of the profession is changing, and this means that librarians should be cautious in advising men that their maleness practically guarantees them a future position of high status or salary. There are relatively more male candidates for these positions than there used to be. Data on the age of respondents illustrate this tendency toward masculinization of the profession. The men are much younger, on the average, than the women. Among the major executives, 40 percent of the men were over fifty years of age as compared with 65 percent of the women. The proportions in the control group are almost identical, 39 and 65 percent, respectively. This means that in both groups, men are replacing women. Here is a case in which it is dangerous to counsel a recruit on the assumption that the future will duplicate the past.

Table 24 supports the proposition that persons persuaded to enter academic librarianship by factors associated with the occupation itself, rather than by extraneous considerations, tend to be highly successful in it. Among members of both sexes, economic, social, or service motivations were reported as influential by major executives more frequently than by other librarians. "Refugee" motivations, desire to escape from another occupation, are reported the most frequently by the control subjects.

TABLE 24.
REASONS FOR CHOOSING LIBRARIANSHIP
AS A CAREER—BY SEX
(CONDENSED TABLE)*

	Male		Female	
Reason Given	Major Executives (142)	Control Group (98)	Major Executives (57)	Control Group (282)
Expediency, chance	34%	23%	21%	29%
Liking for books	21	30	35	28
Liking for people	4	5	17	11
Liking for activities and atmosphere; service opportunity	52	37	53	38
Economic motivation; status of profession; working conditions	33	27	16	12
Refugee from other occupation; use previous training or experience	28	42	33	41
Other†	19	18	30	18

*Did not respond to this question: major executives, male, 27 (16%), female, 5 (8%); control group, male, 15 (13%), female, 70 (20%).

†Condensation of data for this table results in a slight distortion of proportions. It is possible for a subject to have mentioned two or more items within a condensed category. Also a tendency for a "halo" effect is characteristic of tables of this type. In this case it is small: Major executives gave an average of 1.67 reasons per capita; control subjects, 1.46.

That economic motivations are reported more frequently by men than by women is not surprising,[14] but its importance should not be overlooked inasmuch as it is one of the factors accounting for the greater tendency for men than for women to rise in the ranks of almost all occupations.[15] The need for money to support a family is a very strong motivation indeed. Although it is true that many women have aged mothers or other dependents, in general, the goad of financial necessity appears to be much stronger and more widespread among men than among women.

Among men, the desire for economic security and social status overshadows the more general, abstract, and conventional, motivation represented by what Rosenberg calls the "people-oriented" values.[16] Liking for people was mentioned most frequently by female major executives, a group which is also characterized by many and various personal motivations which were difficult to categorize. The female major executive does not entirely fit Rosenberg's model of the "career oriented woman," whom he sees as wanting "to satisfy the values men choose in work rather than the values selected by other women."[17] It appears that the successful woman librarian is an individualist who does not fit any man-imitating stereotype.

Bibliophilism appears to be a frequent motivation for choosing academic librarianship as a career, but it is mentioned less frequently by the subjects of this study than by the library science students queried by the Association of American Library Schools' recruiting committee in 1952.[18] It appears that the administration of a modern library requires more than a basic liking for books and reading. Probably experienced librarians come to realize this and edit their memories of their reasons for choosing the profession accordingly. It may also be that the selection process has weeded out many of the passive book lovers from the relatively elite group represented by this study. The subjects repeatedly point out that an active interest in the relationship between books and people is the important element. A passive love of the smell of old leather and the feel of fine paper may be a desirable cultural attribute in the librarian, but it will solve few of the problems confronting the busy administrator.

A recollection that liking for books prompted one to enter librarianship is more frequently associated with major-executive status among women than among men. The male executive tends to have entered librarianship for more practical reasons, but later in his career he develops a yearning for more contact with books than the press of administrative duties permits. It will indeed be a tragedy if the cares of administration become so heavy that the librarian has little time or energy left for reading, or if a love of books becomes a barrier to attainment of leadership in the profession.

The final topic to be considered in the preprofessional experience of the academic librarian is that of the influence of experience in other occupations. It has been shown here that early experience with academic libraries and librarians is an important ingredient in the personal histories of high-salaried academic librarians. Should one then expect preprofessional experience in another occupation (e.g., schoolteaching) to be an important predictor of future high status in the hierarchical or salary ladders? The data, not reproduced here, are inconclusive on this point. It would appear that for every person for whom the experience or prestige gained in any other occupation was an advantage, there was another who entered librarianship after an unfruitful tenure in another occupation which he either disliked or at which he was not a success.

Approximately one third of the respondents report previous experience with teaching. The percentages for the three groups are as follows: major executives, 34; minor executives, 33; and others, 38. This slight negative tendency is not great enough to justify considering experience as a teacher, per se, a strike against a prospective academic librarian. The point to be considered is whether a candidate turns from teaching to librarianship because he seeks a retreat or because librarianship has greater attractions than teaching.

"ANTICIPATORY SOCIALIZATION": SUMMARY AND COMMENT

Robert K. Merton refers to the process by which one becomes committed to a profession as "socialization."[19] This special application of the term refers to the process of becoming identified with an occupation, of developing an image of oneself as a doctor, lawyer, teacher, etc. Typically, the preliminary phases of this process take place very early in the case of prospective doctors and teachers, later among neophyte lawyers, and even later among future psychologists, social workers, and librarians.

The following factors are thought to be influential in causing people to choose a particular occupation early in life: (1) its visibility, i.e., the extent to which children have experience with people in it, (2) its prestige, and (3) its financial attraction. However, in the case of a profession there is another factor, educational policy. The structure of medical education forces an early decision from prospective doctors.[20] Each premedical course taken increases the student's investment in a medical career. In law, this forced involvement comes somewhat later.[21] In social work,[22] college teaching,[23] and librarianship commitment may be delayed still longer.

The finding that early interest in, and commitment to, librarianship is a predictor of future high status and salary suggests that Herbert Bisno's conclusions concerning social work education be extended to librarianship. These recommendations are:

1. The undergraduate and graduate programs (and the levels within them) should be conceived of as stages within a single program of social work education.
2. Specific content should be required as a prerequisite for admission to graduate schools of social work.
3. Students who have completed a sound undergraduate social work concentration or major should receive preference from the admissions committees of graduate schools of social work.[24]

Bisno feels that "requirements should not be so numerous that making up deficiencies would appear well nigh hopeless" and that this program would not "destroy the autonomy of the liberal arts college and undermine liberal arts education."[25] His position is similar to that of T. R. McConnell and others in advocating that general education and professional training should go on at the same time.[26]

The vestibule requirements for the new-style master's programs of library schools represent a step in the direction recommended by those of Bisno's persuasion. However, it would be necessary to go somewhat further if a true test is to be made of his hypothesis as applied to librarianship. Under this type of program, a further benefit might be the development of a "middle service" made up of (1) graduates of the preliminary undergraduate library science work who chose to work for awhile in preprofessional positions before going on to the full graduate program, and (2) those who chose to remain in subprofessional positions permanently.

The findings here definitely fail to support Everett Hughes' hypothesis that professions on the level of librarianship "are going to regret their attempts to force down the age of crucial decision to enter or not to enter the occupation" even though the older professions, such as medicine, have done so.[27] To support Hughes' position, data would be required showing that leadership of the library profession tends to come from among those who decided to enter late in life. Although the differences are not large, all the data here are in the opposite direction from that required by Hughes' hypothesis. Nevertheless, Hughes' remarks on this subject are pertinent even though the data here fail to support his main contention:

> There is a good deal to be said for the good maverick, the person with a high degree of intellectual curiosity and energy who changes her or his mind or did not make it up early. In

the early days of a profession the leaders, that is, the founders, are generally enthusiastic mavericks. And it is always a question of how much a profession gains by becoming conventional, rigid, and unfriendly to the maverick.[28]

The conclusion would seem to be that professions like librarianship should, to continue the cattle-ranch analogy, select good young stock early but not refuse the late-developing mavericks. Recruits who have "a high degree of intellectual curiosity and energy" may be found in either the early- or late-choosing group, but, in general, selection is likely to be better before the herd has been picked over by cowhands from other ranches.

To say that students should be presented with librarianship as a career choice early in the game is not to recommend that late entrants be barred. The Joint Committee on Librarianship as a Career has expressed the implications of the data presented here in the following declaration:

Be sure that the "refugee" from another field—the ex-school teacher, ex-lawyer, or ex-whatever—is really suitable for library work and not just a "refugee" from everything.[29]

IN-SERVICE FACTORS

The social status of a person's family, his own educational background, the time at which he decided to enter librarianship, and his reasons for doing so have all been shown to have some bearing on the subsequent course of the academic librarian's career. Once he has been admitted to the fold, there are still other choices to be made and influences brought to bear on the course of his experience. These factors will now be considered.

In considering these in-service factors, two unresolved dilemmas must be kept in mind. (1) Many in-service choices are not really new "decisions" but merely the results of things that happened earlier, perhaps even before the librarian was born. (2) In evaluating a person's achievement, it is impossible to separate the influence of the availability of opportunity from the ability or willingness to take advantage of it. Unfortunately, in a profession short of personnel, it may well be that willingness to make a change or to accept an office may be more important than capacity to do the job or to perform the duties of the office. The factors shaping the course of a person's life are subtle, complex, and intertwined, but this should not deter the investigator from attempting to isolate and examine a few of these forces.

54   The Career of the Academic Librarian

OBTAINING A POSITION

His first position is of obvious importance to the subsequent achievement of a librarian. Accordingly, the means by which he obtains this and subsequent positions is of considerable significance in the development of an effective corps of manpower for the profession.

Table 25 gives some information about how librarians obtain their first and subsequent positions. The principle finding here will be news to practically no one: the better jobs are not secured through formal channels. However, at least on the lower levels, the market for librarians appears to be more "open" than that for teaching personnel described in *The Academic Marketplace*.[30] For securing a first position, the placement services of library schools seem to be well regarded. Presumably these are agencies that place emphasis on "what" rather than "who" you know, but beyond this, more subtle means of placement are employed.

TABLE 25.
HELP RECEIVED BY SUBJECTS IN OBTAINING
POSITIONS IN LIBRARIES*

Type of Help	Major Executives (213)	Minor Executives (226)	Others (238)	Total (677)
Placement services of a library school	51%	50%	47%	49%
Other placement services and agencies	9	13	12	12
Advertisements and notices	8	10	6	8
Letters of inquiry to prospective employers	17	19	24	20
Individual contacts through friends and associates	77‡	63	54	65
Other	8	10	11	10

Proportions of Subjects Who Received Some or Much Help from Each Agency or Method†

*Information lacking for 30 subjects.
†Percentages total more than 100 because respondents were free to mark as many items as they chose.
‡Difference between major executives and combined control group significant at .01 level.

The most significant thing about the subjects' reaction to the placement process is their apathy toward it.[31] Although many criticized what they regard as an unwarranted tendency to appoint "bright young men" without experience to top jobs, they have virtually nothing to say about the placement process responsible for this state of affairs. It may well be that the average academic librarian is only nominally interested in advancement in the hierarchy, particularly if this means moving to another locality deemed less climatically or culturally attractive. Those desiring more responsible technical positions (e.g., specialists in the more difficult aspects of cataloging) have long been in a seller's market and need little help in finding new positions. Those who are in the minority interested in "getting ahead" and "rising to the top of the heap" are confident of their own ability to make themselves visible to prospective employers without relying on placement agencies. Such librarians seem content to rely on "director recommendation by leading librarian-associates" (librarian of a large university), "becoming known to the profession through publishing" (director of libraries of a large university), or "pure luck—being at the right place at the right time" (university librarian of a medium-sized institution).

To carry this speculation a point further, it might be argued that this lack of interest in the placement process may reflect the incomplete transition of academic librarianship from a clerical occupation to a responsible, self-regulating profession. Schoolteachers are in a similar position.[32] It is true that librarianship has been professionalized beyond the labor-management dichotomy symbolized by a hiring-hall kind of placement. On the other hand, the college professor has progressed further than the academic librarian in securing a voice in the determination of his own destiny, although there are many anomalies in his position too.[33]

It is true that the American Library Association has delved into matters of personnel selection and has tried at various times to maintain a placement service,[34] but the manpower policy in the profession is as liberal and constructive as it is, due to the work of an oligarchy of chief librarians without much help from other members of the profession.

VARIETY OF EXPERIENCE

In a very lucid article on the place of experience in developing college and university librarians, E. W. McDiarmid contends:

> ...there are three important factors in the development of library leaders: (1) personal qualities and characteristics;

(2) proper education, both academic and professional; and (3) adequate experience.... The ideally qualified librarian would be a person with high-grade mental and personality qualities, adequately developed and sharpened by education, and applied, tested and demonstrated by experience.[35]

The role of experience has been extensively studied by Harvey.[36] He examined in detail job mobility and its correlates in the careers of the 1,316 chief librarians listed in the 1943 edition of *Who's Who in Library Service*. He found that variety of experience is, to a degree, correlated with upward mobility in the ranks of college and university librarians, but he feels, in the light of McDiarmid's hypothesis, that the correlation ought to be stronger. Of the chief college and university librarians he studied, Harvey states:

[they] had reached administrative positions of responsibility without the benefit of an enriching variety of experience. However, a minority of this group had had varied experience, in some cases quite varied, and we may be thankful for this minority.[37]

The data gathered from the 1958 librarians relate to only one aspect of variety of experience, viz., the number of libraries in which the subjects have worked. In general, the conclusion is that the 1958 group of chief librarians has had a greater variety of experience than a comparable group of subjects in 1943. In 1958 it was almost essential that a librarian have worked in at least two libraries during his career if his last position is to be that of major executive. Only twenty-eight major executives reported experience in only one library, and most of them had been appointed directly from professorial ranks rather than promoted from the library staff. The chief executives tend to have moved much more frequently than members of the minor-executive group. The latter were, in turn, somewhat more mobile than the nonexecutives.

Table 26 summarizes the mobility data on the 1958 group as compared with the college and university portion of Harvey's subjects. The 1958 group of chief academic librarians, both male and female, have had more varied experience than the 1943 group, insofar as number of libraries in which they have worked is a measure of this. The difference cannot be explained away on the basis that the 1958 group is older (median age 50) than the 1943 group (median age 43).[38] Among the 1958 academic librarians under fifty years of age, the proportion of major executives who worked in four or more libraries is 58 percent compared to 26 percent for

TABLE 26.
MOBILITY: NUMBER OF LIBRARIES IN WHICH SUBJECTS HAVE
HELD FULL-TIME POSITIONS—RELATED TO POSITION AND SEX*

	Male		Female		
Number of Libraries in Which Positions Have Been Held	Major Executives (161)	Control Group (106)	Major Executives (60)	Control Group (339)	Head College Librarians 1943† (639)
One to three	46%	68%	50%	64%	74%
Four or more	54	32	50	36	26

*Information lacking for 41 subjects.
†John F. Harvey, *The Librarian's Career: A Study of Mobility* ("ACRL Microcard Series," No.85 [Rochester, N.Y.: Univ. of Rochester Press]), p.167. The term "College Librarian" includes "University Librarian" also.

Harvey's group. Furthermore, whereas Harvey found variety of experience to correlate positively with age, there was a negative tendency in the 1958 group. Despite having had more time to do so, those fifty years of age or older tended to have moved less frequently than their younger colleagues. The conclusion is inescapable: variety of experience is a more prominent feature of the careers of chief academic librarians in 1958 than it was of those in the 1940's. The virtually closed job market of the depression probably kept Harvey's subjects from acquiring varied experience.

Harvey makes a point of his finding that, among both public and academic librarians, men tend to have had a more varied experience than women. He concludes:

> ...there is no question but that men were better prepared by their experience for administration and for top-level positions than were women, no matter how capable they were, nor how much more innate ability they may have had.[39]

In interpreting the above statement, it is well to remember that no matter how willing a person may be to move to another more enriching experience, he (or, in this case, she) must have the opportunity to do so. It may be true that one of the reasons women do not advance in the library profession as frequently as men do is to be found in unwillingness on the part of women to move from place to place, but neither Harvey's nor the present data bear directly on this question. Nor does Harvey explicitly draw the conclusion that women are unwilling to move in order to achieve positions of leadership, but others have read this into his writings.[40]

58   The Career of the Academic Librarian

While data from the 1958 academic librarians do not settle this question, they do shed some light on it. It is true that, in total, the men have moved more often than the women, but Table 26 shows that when position level is, as the statisticians term it, "held constant," the proportion of men with "variety of experience" is not impressively greater than that of women, a matter of four percentage points. To put it another way, there are virtually as many women as men in the control group with experience in several libraries, but despite this, we are very safe in assuming that a greater number of men will become chief executives. Thus, Harvey's conclusions for the 1943 group do not hold in 1958.

This is even more evident when one examines the association between mobility and salary in the control group. The following tabulation shows the percentage of members of the control group (minor executives and those without extensive administrative responsibilities) who have held positions in four or more libraries:

Among those earning less than $6000 a year:
          Males   29
          Females   33
Among those earning $6000 or more a year:
          Males   35
          Females   41

In the first place, it will be noted that the association is much weaker between variety of experience and salary than between it and hierarchical position (shown in Table 26). In the second place, in both salary categories, the proportion of mobile females is greater than the proportion of males! Insofar as experience in several libraries is a desirable attribute for promotion, there were proportionately more women than men eligible for advancement. In the third place, although there is some tendency in that direction, it would appear that women have used mobility somewhat less than they have education (as exemplified in the tabulation of holders of second professional degrees) as a means of overcoming the disadvantages which females experience in securing advancement in a man's world. Although they have had as great a variety of experience as men, women, because of marital and other factors, are not able to take advantage of it.

All of this does not invalidate the central hypothesis of Harvey and McDiarmid.[41] Whether salary or position be taken as the criterion of success, mobility is a correlate of it. The data here tend to give strong support to the hypothesis that opportunity to move and willingness to take advantage of the opportunity rank with "personal qualities and characteristics" and with "proper education, both academic and professional" as characteristics of those who should, and in 1958 did, lead the profession. There may well be many "mute inglorious Miltons" in academic librarianship who have failed to make a maximum contribution because personal ties and habits of mind kept them from going to the place where opportunity lay or from accepting responsibilities proffered. On the other hand, as Lipset and Bendix have pointed out, those who continually burn their bridges behind them sometimes pay a high psychological price for the "success" they achieve.[42] More will be said of this later.

PARTICIPATION IN VOLUNTARY ASSOCIATIONS

The proposition to be demonstrated here is that, whereas participation in professional and scholarly organizations is directly correlated with a librarian's position and salary, activity in community organizations is not.

Tables 27 through 29 indicate that, in general, academic librarians are very active in professional and scholarly organizations but somewhat less concerned with groups not intimately associated with the practice of librarianship. However, on both counts, the academic librarians are more active than the librarians studied by the Public Library Inquiry. Whereas only 3 percent of the academic librarians report no memberships in professional and scholarly organizations, the proportion of public librarians, though not specifically given, appears to have been much higher.[43] In the case of community organizations, 20 percent of the academic librarians reported no membership compared to "about half" of the public librarians;[44] even greater differences are found when office holding is the level of participation considered.[45]

TABLE 27.
ACTIVITY IN PROFESSIONAL AND SCHOLARLY ORGANIZATIONS*

Type of Activity	Major Executives (230)	Minor Executives (228)	Others (238)
Membership in two or more organizations	98%	91%	79%
Attendance at meetings of two or more organizations	85	70	48
Service on committees of two or more organizations	64	45	24
Officer or committee chairmanship in two or more organizations	47	29	16

*Information lacking for 11 subjects.

TABLE 28.
ACTIVITY IN PROFESSIONAL AND SCHOLARLY ORGANIZATIONS
RELATED TO SALARY*

Type of Activity	Major Executives Less than $8000 (105)	Major Executives $8000 or More (125)	Control Group Less than $6000 (293)	Control Group $6000 or More (168)
Membership in two or more organizations	100%	97%	82%	91%
Attendance at meetings of two or more organizations	80	87	53	70
Service on committees of two or more organizations	51	75	27	45
Officer or committee chairmanship in two or more organizations	38	53	16	35

*Information lacking for 11 subjects.

Academic librarians are "joiners." Their record compares very favorably with other groups that enjoy relatively high social status. For example, Scott's study of membership in voluntary associations among residents of Bennington, Vermont, indicates that the mean number of memberships per capita for the population generally was 1.67; for college graduates it was 2.72; and for the upper social classes, 3.23.[46] The corresponding figure for academic librarians is 5.3. Making allowance for a differing treatment of church membership in the two studies (subtract about .5 from the figure for librarians), it still appears that the average academic librarian belongs to more organizations than does the average member of any of the groups studied by Scott.

The predominent record for membership and office holding among academic librarians is in professional and scholarly associations. It would appear that members of the college and university segment of the library profession, to a greater extent than the public library portion, agree with the National Education Association's statement of the importance of professional organizations:

> These associations form an essential part of professional life; they give expression to the solidarity of the profession and perform services which a profession requires and which cannot be performed by individuals alone.[47]

Following the lead of the pioneer, Emile Durkheim, sociologists have continually placed great emphasis on voluntary organizations as characteristic of a "plural democracy" as opposed to a "mass society."[48] On the other hand, Devereux and Weiner, in commenting on the nursing profession, call attention to another aspect of "joining":

> ...for fear of being "down-graded" socially and equated with the "upper-lower-classes"...the nurse is sometimes compelled to starch the facade of her professionalism even more than she starches her uniform.[49]

However, if professionalism among academic librarians stems from a pathological concern about status, this is not revealed in the responses to the questionnaire used in the present study.

Just as in other segments of the population, participation in general community organizations by librarians appears to be "a sometime thing for some people."[50] Even so, the extent of such participation among academic librarians is at least equal to that in other segments of the social class to which members of the salaried professions belong.[51] However, respondents made no remarks at all about community participation in the free-comment sections of the questionnaire. Apparently they consider such activity a private matter not within the scope of their role as professional people.
In the Public Library Inquiry, at least some of the subjects seemed to recognize a close affinity between community organizations and the public library.[52] Given this closer relationship in the case of the public, as compared with the academic, library, the fact that the record of community participation is higher among academic than public librarians gives added weight to the dissatisfaction expressed by the Inquiry staff concerning lack of interest in community organizations among public librarians in 1947.[53]

In contrast to participation in professional and scholarly organizations, activity in religious, civic, fraternal, or social organizations is not strongly associated with either high status or salary in the profession (Table 29). This somewhat surprising tendency can also be seen in the data presented, but not analysed, by Carson for California accountants.[54] Zeal in professional matters is part of the role of the academic library executive (or would-be executive), whereas the librarian who is either not interested in advancement in the hierarchy, or who has given up hope of it, may feel that dues paid to professional organizations are a waste of money for the rank and file. Some of these nonexecutives probably find satisfaction from participation or leadership in community activity that they do not find in their professional careers and carefully keep the two aspects of their lives separate.

TABLE 29.
ACTIVITY IN COMMUNITY ORGANIZATIONS*

(Respondents were asked to give activity in religious, civic, fraternal, or social organizations.)

Type of Activity	Major Executives (226)	Minor Executives (229)	Others (238)
Membership in two or more organizations	57%	58%	53%
Attendance at meetings of two or more organizations	26	26	24
Service on committees of two or more organizations	20	18	17
Officer or committee chairmanship in two or more organizations	16	15	12

*Information lacking for 14 subjects. In general, it should be noted that many subjects seemed not to understand the question or not to be interested in answering it fully.

The strong association of hierarchical and salary status (Table 28) with active participation in professional organization indicates a tendency toward oligarchy about which the American Library Association worries considerably. From time to time, the Association strives mightily to extend "grass roots participation."[55] This is a battle against a tendency Robert Michels called the "iron law of oligarchy" in organizational affairs. However, there are organizations which have successfully shown that this "law" is not necessarily "iron."[56]

A number of the factors Lipset, Trow, and Coleman found to be associated with democratic participation in the International Typographical Union are applicable to professional organizations, including those of librarians.[57] For example: (1) "The less internally stratified an occupation, the greater the chances for democracy in its union." Perhaps as an occupation makes the transition from a quasi-clerical to a fully professional status, the stratification within the ranks of the professional segment will decrease, even as the cleavage from the clerical and technical levels becomes sharper. Thus, the American Library Association may become an exclusively professional organization rather than one purporting to embrace everyone who works in a library. Presumably, within this narrower frame of reference, participation by the rank and file would increase. Other organizations would arise to care for the needs of the technical and clerical library worker. (2) The greater the "number and variety of functions" an organization performs, the greater the interest and participation among its members. The American Library Association and other library associations have engaged in very heterogenous programs that have not, however, reached the rank and file to the extent desired. (3) As library staffs grow larger, librarians will have more opportunity to "socialize with one another informally on and around the job," a factor found to be favorable to organizational democracy. Geographical isolation of small college library staffs can be combatted by the development of vigorous regional, state, and district library organizations and by provision of money for travel to professional conferences. (4) The opening of many channels of communication is said to increase democracy in an organization. For a profession as geographically scattered as academic librarianship, this means that the publication media available are of considerable importance. This will be the subject of the next section.

PUBLISH OR PERISH?

The influence of publication on the career of the academic man has been discussed so frequently that it need not be reviewed here.[58] It would appear that the tenure of the nonadministrative librarian is not so directly dependent upon having the results of his intellectual labors appear in print as is that of his colleague on the teaching faculty. Nevertheless, the fact that it is expected of those in positions of responsibility in academic libraries has been well established by previous research.[59]

The body of published writing produced by the group of academic librarians who responded to the present study is considerable (Table 30). As expected, the number of publications a librarian has to his credit is strongly associated with the level of position he holds and with the salary he receives. Publication is primarily a masculine phenomenon and its correlation with position and salary is much stronger among men than among women. This may be a function of the greater drive of men to get ahead in the profession (discussed in connection with Table 24 above) and of their greater identification with the teaching faculty (primarily a masculine society).[60] Also, the men have done more research work toward advanced degrees than the women and thus have more raw material upon which to base publications. Table 30 shows that the gap between the publication records of men and women is large among both the major executives and the control subjects. Nor is this an activity used to any extent by ambitious women to overcome

TABLE 30.
NUMBER OF PUBLICATIONS

Number of Items Published	Male Major Executives (169)	Male Control Group (113)	Female Major Executives (62)	Female Control Group (252)
None reported	7%	32%	29%	46%
One to three	30	25	39	36
Four to nine	27	27	23	12
Nine or less	63	44	33	18
Ten or more	36	17	10	6

the inherent disadvantage of being a woman. Female major executives have not published as frequently as male members of the control group.

Among members of the control group, publication rate is related to type of position held. Administrative personnel (without major-executive status) and branch or special collections librarians are the most prolific, and technical processes people the least. The catalog and acquisitions librarians have taken steps to remedy this situation by expanding the already excellent *Journal of Cataloging and Classification* into *Library Resources and Technical Services,* an exemplary publication. The function of publications such as this is, of course, to further the communication of ideas within the profession, but probably of almost equal importance is their ability to encourage and make visible talent that otherwise might lie dormant.

As is the case with other factors in the career pattern of librarians, it is impossible to tell from the data whether publication, scholarly or professional, is chicken or egg. Is publication something one does after he has "arrived" (i.e., is it part of the role one plays in an executive position) or is it instrumental in the process of arriving at such a position? No doubt both are involved. Some of the comments of "elder statesmen" indicate that the pressure for preparing material for publication eases a bit during the later phases of one's career.

Librarianship is fortunate in having outlets for those who wish to say something in print. The danger exists, however, that librarians will overemphasize this factor, as teaching faculty members are frequently alleged to have done. Caplow states the extreme case:

> ...for most members of the academic teaching profession, the real strain in the academic role arises from the fact that they

are, in essence, paid to do one job, whereas the worth of their services is evaluated on the basis of how well they do another.[61]

The data gathered here do not suggest that this has happened to any extent in academic librarianship. Several subjects commented to the effect that if more librarians engaged in scholarly (as opposed to administrative or technical) research and writing, the status of the profession would be improved and the ability of its members to render good service enhanced. However, none commented on the possibility of publication becoming a mere ritual practiced by those who seek higher status in the academic community. At any rate, the data summarized in Table 30 may be cited by those seeking academic rank for librarians to show that librarians do, in fact, publish. Even the least productive group, the female control-group category, can point to the fact that more than half of its members have published something during the course of their careers.

REACTION TO LIBRARY WORK

Academic librarians are critical of their occupation, but few of them regret having entered it. This is evident in the following tabulation. It shows the proportions of various occupational groups expressing regret at having chosen each particular line of work:

Various occupations[62]		35%
Business and professional people[63]		20%
Teachers (New York)[64]		24%
Teachers (southern United States)[65]		22%
College faculty members (Minnesota)[66]		17%
Professional public librarians[67]		26%
Illinois librarians[68]		11%
Academic librarians		13%
Major executives	13%	
Minor executives	10%	
Others	14%	

These figures are based upon somewhat different phrasing of the question and treatment of the answers. In the case of the academic librarians, any uncertainty was counted as dissatisfaction. Thus, it is clear that academic librarians are considerably less prone to express dissatisfaction with their occupational choice than other professional people. The difference between the dissatisfaction rate of academic librarians and that of working people generally is rather dramatic.

Among public librarians, the Inquiry found that "the higher the professional position achieved, the more likely the person is to feel that his vocational choice was wise."[69] The situation among academic librarians is different: Members of the middle level are the least likely to express dissatisfaction with their choice of this profession. As might be expected, members of the middle group also tended to write statements indicating the strongest dedication to the profession. The major executives sometimes expressed a feeling that, while they had done well in librarianship, they might have achieved an even greater success in some other field, i.e., that librarianship imposed a ceiling on their ambitions.

The various sources of satisfaction academic librarians say they find in their work are summarized in Table 31. The four principal ones will be discussed here in order of popularity:

1. Half of the subjects indicate that they found service to people the most attractive feature of their work. This tends to be a stereotyped answer both to the question "Why did you choose librarianship?" and "What do you like best about it now?" However, it is significant to note that the proportions giving this answer to these two questions differ. The "service to people" emphasis was given by only 21 percent of the subjects in stating their reasons for choosing librarianship, in contrast to the 50 percent who now find it their greatest source of satisfaction. From this it seems clear that for many librarians, appreciation for librarianship as a public-service activity develops after they enter the profession rather than being a reason for choosing it. As would be expected, this source of satisfaction is most prevalent among those librarians whose task it is to serve the public directly. However, 28 percent of the technical processes people also mentioned it. As one cataloger put it, they derive their satisfaction from playing a "part in creating a tool which is useful to scholars." This is undoubtedly a sincere expression of the old principle of the bricklayer building a cathedral and should be emphasized in recruiting technical processes librarians. It should be noted that this service motive, a distinguishing mark of the professional person, is also strongly felt by teaching faculty members in colleges and universities. Respondents to the Minnesota study of faculty members mention various activities connected with teaching students much more frequently than those connected with research.[70]

The "service to people" interest is particularly strong among female librarians, whereas they seldom find major satisfaction in their relations with colleagues. Furthermore, the service emphasis tends to distinguish women with major-executive status from other women, but this tendency is not found to any extent among the men.

2. The second-ranking source of satisfactions, "Work with books;

TABLE 31.
FACTORS LIKED BEST ABOUT LIBRARY WORK*

(These are free-response items.)

Factor Mentioned	Male Major Executives (161)	Male Control Group (110)	Female Major Executives (62)	Female Control Group (335)	All Subjects (668)
Service to people	46%	42%	71%	52%	50%
Work with books; build collections	33	25	24	21	24
Technical and precise work	2	14	2	14	10
Stimulating environment and interesting colleagues	19	13	6	18	17
Opportunity to learn and do research	9	17	6	13	12
Training and supervision of staff; personnel work	2	4	-	2	2
Problem solving; specialized bibliographic work	4	13	10	16	12
Administration and planning	26	10	24	6	13
Good working conditions; security	3	4	-	2	3
Variety of work experience	7	5	8	6	6
Other	13	11	5	5	8

*Information lacking for 39 subjects (i.e., mentioned no factors). Significance of difference not tested.

build collections," is also a stereotyped response in many instances, but, like the service emphasis, it is given more frequently in this connection than it is as a motive for entering librarianship. It also exhibits an interesting sex reversal. Among major executives, the women tend to give a bibliophilic answer to the question about reasons for entering librarianship, whereas the men mention it as a source of satisfaction. Among male executives, there is a certain wistfulness about their mention of obtaining satisfactions through work with books. Several of them felt that, although this was what they enjoyed most, it was what they did least. Many of the male major executives entered the profession because it offered them a chance to get ahead, to exercise leadership in administration. Now, having achieved this goal, they tend to yearn for some of the bibliographic pleasures that the pressure of administrative duties has prevented them from tasting to the desired extent.

3. The third-ranking source of satisfaction is "Stimulating environment and interesting colleagues." It is mentioned to some extent among all groups except the female major executives. The female major executive sees other faculty members in a "service to people" context and finds it a source of satisfaction but, being excluded from this masculine society, does not view teaching faculty members as colleagues.

In general, librarians do not find satisfactions derived from colleagues as frequently as do teaching faculty members. These findings confirm empirically the contentions set forth in Knapp's penetrating essay on the sociology of college librarianship.[71] Knapp points out that the task of establishing a colleague relationship with members of the academic community while still maintaining it with other librarians is very difficult and frustrating.

4. The major executives account for much of the popularity enjoyed by "administration and planning" as a source of satisfaction, but only a quarter of them mentioned it. Furthermore, as indicated above, the major executive complains that, although he likes this phase of library work, it tends to separate him from bibliographic activity which remains his first love. Nor do middle managers seem to care much for the administrative responsibilities that result from separating the various levels of work in well-managed libraries. They seem to feel that the administrative and "intellectual" aspects of the profession are antagonistic rather than parts of a coordinated whole.

Those involved in recruiting for the profession will see in the totals column of Table 31 ample justification for "selling" librarianship as a social rather than a solitary occupation. Although it is true that "social integrity" and ability "to work easily with people"[72] are of utmost importance in library work, the service lure must be presented carefully. As one respondent put it:

> Library school training seems to emphasize the joys of reader's service at the expense of technical services. This is a mistake, I think, for libraries could not exist without order librarians, serials librarians, catalogers, etc. Graduates of library schools are amazed to find out that cataloging, for example, can be interesting. There must be some way that library school instructors can put the idea across to their students that there are joys in all kinds of library work instead of prejudicing them in favor of one type of work and against other types.

That the modal category of things liked least about library work should be "Nonprofessional duties, routine" will surprise no one (Table 32). Only the head librarians of large libraries, who have large staffs to which these duties may be delegated, are comparatively free of this complaint.

Lack of distinction between professional and nonprofessional duties is a perennial source of discontent among practitioners of professions that are on about the same level as librarianship (e.g., social work[73] and elementary education[74]). The problem is not a simple one. In the first place, "routine appears to be a subjective reaction to a particular type of activity and is not inherent in the activity itself."[75] In the second place, there is a tendency for professional workers to favor separation of clerical from professional duties in general, but not in particular.[76] Proposals to relieve the professional worker of tasks that would seem to be of a subprofessional nature are often strenuously resisted. This resistance may stem from a subconscious feeling that the professional monopoly of the art is threatened or that the continuity of service will be broken. Heathcote, writing in the *Library Journal* about a controversy concerning the need for a middle service in librarianship, says:

> It seems to me that there is a very real place for undergraduate library courses, and if we're so afraid these people will displace us, perhaps there is reason for soul searching on our part.[77]

The subjects of the present study would seem to agree with Heathcote's contention. It is encouraging to find that, at least among members of this relatively elite segment of the library profession, there is little fear expressed that subprofessional workers will

TABLE 32.
FACTORS LIKED LEAST ABOUT LIBRARY WORK*
(These are free-response items.)

	Male		Female		
Factor Mentioned	Major Executives (145)	Control Group (102)	Major Executives (55)	Control Group (313)	All Subjects (615)
Administrative detail; red tape†	21%	22%	29%	15%	19%
Personnel administration and problems with staff	22	24	13	9	15
Nonprofessional duties, routine	10	30	27	30	25
Problems with readers; reference work generally	12	13	7	7	9
Working conditions; pressure of work	6	8	11	18	13
Low salary and lack of opportunity for advancement	5	7	2	4	5
Status of profession; lack of understanding on part of public	9	6	5	4	6
Technical processes; detail work	8	7	16	16	13
Financial problems of libraries	12	3	5	1	4
Formal public relations (e.g., speeches)	3	-	2	1	1
Other factors‡	9	13	2	13	11

*Information lacking for 92 subjects (i.e., mentioned no factors). Significance of differences not tested.
†Includes aversion to questionnaires.
‡Includes highly subjective statements and "pet peeves" that could not be classified elsewhere.

encroach upon professional prerogatives. On the other hand, such fears may be something one feels but dares not express.

It is a mistake to assume that the problem of distinction between levels of work is restricted to "emerging" professions such as elementary education, social work, and librarianship. The Minnesota study of faculty members in four-year colleges found "Too much red tape and routine duties" to be one of "two or three major dissatisfactions experienced" in faculty service.[78]

The proportion of Minnesota college faculty members who complain about poor salary (47 percent)[79] is as startlingly high as that of academic librarians is unexpectedly low (5 percent). Nor can this be explained by difference in sex composition of the two groups. Among male librarians, the highest proportion mentioning salary is only 7 percent. The average salary of faculty members in Minnesota in 1958 was certainly higher than that of the librarians without major-executive status.[80] Yet the librarians complain much less frequently about salary. Why?

A superficial explanation would be that librarians have fewer or less-demanding dependents than do college professors, and this may be true in some cases. However, it would seem that one must dig deeper than this for an explanation. Speculation might take one or more of the following courses: (1) Librarians are more concerned about working conditions and division of labor than are professors and, hence, are distracted from expending their venom on the salary problem. (2) It would be flattering to librarians if they could say that they are more frequently dedicated to the service ideal than are faculty members, and thus they spend their reforming zeal on problems of the profession rather than on their own economic status (the professoriate would certainly object to this hypothesis!). (3) Perhaps the style of life required of the teaching faculty member is more expensive to maintain than that demanded of the librarian and, hence, the financial pressures differ. (4) A personality variable may be involved. Are professors a more aggressive and candid lot than librarians? Can the librarian be stereotyped as a dedicated, self-effacing, self-depreciating introvert who considers it "unprofessional" to talk about money? (Some light will be shed on this point in the chapter on personality, Chapter V.) (5) Being a relatively small, socially and administratively isolated group, academic librarians may have no standard, no point of reference, by which to judge the adequacy of their salaries.

Sociologists and social psychologists in "the new and rapidly expanding field of reference group analysis"[81] would favor the last explanation.

> [Reference-group analysis] is concerned with the "determinants and consequences of those processes of evaluation and self-appraisal in which the individual takes the values or

or standards of *other individuals and groups as a comparative frame of reference.*"[82]

It may be that, despite the wish of leaders of the profession to equate librarianship with academic teaching, many ordinary librarians appear not to espouse the teaching faculty as their "reference group." It should be recalled, in this connection, that the group studied here is the "older generation." As more and more libraries grant formal faculty status to librarians, the identification pattern may well change.

The reference-group perception of the average librarian is no doubt clouded and confused. He is a member of an isolated group. While he may have *de jure* faculty rank, he is conscious of not having that status *de facto*. On the other hand, he definitely does not consider himself a member of the clerical or custodial staff of the institution. Thus, the average librarian, once he gets into a salary bracket above mere subsistence, cannot point to any other occupation that is comparable and say, "They are getting more than we for doing work of similar status." He simply does not know what status his work does enjoy and thus has no basis on which to formulate a logical "grievance" about salary. By contrast, the American Association of University Professors has done a practical sort of reference-group analysis for the teaching faculty member to the extent that it has been accused of "trade union practice."[83]

Personnel administration is third in rank on the list of things that trouble academic librarians. Furthermore, few subjects expressed a liking for this phase of librarianship (Table 31). This complaint is much more frequent among men than among women. This may be partially explained by saying that more of the men than of the women are involved in directing the work of others, but this does not explain the responses of men in nonexecutive positions. Male librarians are a minority group in the profession. A favored minority, perhaps, but still a minority. Thus, in relationships with the rest of the staff, the men find what they perceive to be "pettiness," "jealousy," and "personal friction." Some of this may be a reaction to the anomalous status of librarians. The ambitious man, to whom much has been promised in librarianship, finds himself "under natural status pressure...to identify with the academic world rather than the library world."[84] Thus, he may find himself out of sympathy with those who continue to identify with the library world, and consider their attitudes "petty." Lest this speculation acquire too psychoanalytic a tone, it should be pointed out that many of the subjects in executive positions dislike personnel administration out of a simple humanitarian dislike of having to discipline or fire employees.

It was surprising to find that only 6 percent of the subjects expressed concern about problems of status. Public school teachers, for example, are not so reticent on this point.[85] Weak reference-group identification is certainly involved here just as it was in the case of apparent lack of concern over salary. However, it may well be that being from high-status backgrounds in the first place, academic librarians are not chronic "status seekers." Although small, the group exhibiting status anxiety is very articulate and sometimes bitter. As a suggestion for improving librarianship, one assistant librarian advocated:

> ... *vigorous* but *selective* recruitment to obtain prospects who will undo the harm done by the stereotype; i.e. who do not consider *salary* and *status* "dirty words," who are not escaping from life, who are proud of their profession.

A head librarian advocates emulation of other professions:

> ...we must not only aim at the same salaries as the professors do but aim to have the same attitudes toward higher learning that they usually have. We must set our sights higher and concern ourselves less with those routines that clerical workers will handle as well or better than we can. Only in that fashion will we gain the kind of respect enjoyed by judges, doctors, engineers, etc. Nobody in the world cares for those librarians who are only interested in gadgets and techniques. The best in our profession are highly cultured and broadly educated people; let us try to emulate them.

On the other side of the argument, a branch librarian may be speaking for many of those who did not indicate concern about status. He expresses the "separate-but-equal" doctrine in this manner:

> The librarian should be trained and also be so constituted as to be proud of his position as a librarian. He should not attempt to achieve importance by associating his activities with other fields, such as teaching. The librarian, if anything, is a teacher in the library, and as such is playing a very important role in the educational process. The leader in the library field could be a leader in any other field if properly trained. Leadership isn't confined to one profession, it is characteristic only of certain people. Librarians should not be ashamed of their profession.

If librarians on many campuses occupy not a low status, but, rather, no status at all, the respondents appear to feel that this is something members of a genteel calling do not discuss, even on an anonymous questionnaire. Some may even value this anomalous status as a refuge from the stresses to which the status seeker is subjected. One very articulate female librarian, who holds a doctorate in a subject field, declared:

> I have enjoyed my life as a librarian, and I know I would choose it again if I had to make the choice—all factors being equal to those in 1925. We have less vacation and a *great deal less* salary than the professors, but we do have less concentrated work, in that we do not stand on a platform and give lectures. Therefore, I believe that we keep younger longer and do not wear out our nerves. (I still have 12 years to go!)

The lesson here seems to be that those who are trying to secure the explicit symbols of status, especially academic rank, for librarians will get only passive support from many of their colleagues. On the other hand, those concerned with elevating the status of librarians comprise a very vigorous and articulate group.

SUMMARY

Among academic librarians, early consideration of, and commitment to, librarianship as a career is associated with high future status and salary. Implications are not that older people and those who, for want of a better term, are called refugees from other occupations should be excluded, but, rather, that early commitment should be encouraged.

Those who choose librarianship through the influence connected with academic libraries and librarians are more frequently successful in rising in the hierarchy than those influenced by public library or nonlibrary factors. Economic and status motivations for entering librarianship are more frequently characteristic of men than of women.

Lower-level positions, especially beginning positions, are obtained through formal channels, but the better-paid and higher-status places are secured by other, less formal, contacts. Mobility, "variety of experience," is increasingly characteristic of academic librarians as time goes by. Probably because of fewer opportunities to make upward moves, female librarians tend to be less mobile than male. However, women who do achieve executive status tend to make more moves in the process than do their male colleagues in similar positions. Participation in professional organizations is a distinguishing feature of librarians in the higher hierarchical or salaried positions, but the rate of community participation is about the same for all levels. Publication is a more conspicuous feature of the role of a top executive than of a nonexecutive, of a man than of a woman. A gratifying number of librarians publish their ideas and the results of their research. However, "publish or perish" is not yet a phrase applicable to librarianship.

Academic librarians' reactions to their work reflect their position in the hierarchy and, to an extent, the type of work they do. Realization that librarianship is a social profession develops after a person has entered it and is not frequently recalled as being a motive for entering. The colleague relationship is a source of satisfaction among male top executives and among females in other categories. Female chief executives are relatively isolated on the campus and compensate for this by developing a client, rather than colleague, relationship as a source of satisfaction. Impatience with nonprofessional duties is endemic among academic librarians. However, this is a frequent complaint among college and university teachers also. Development of a better-trained subprofessional stratum for librarianship is favored by respondents to this study. If any of them fear that this would encroach upon valued prerogatives, they did not admit it.

Academic librarianship is a satisfying occupation for an overwhelming majority of its practitioners. They assure bright young people that this is an intellectually stimulating profession, that it is "people oriented," and that if they had it to do over they would again become librarians.

NOTES

[1] Alice I. Bryan, *The Public Librarian: A Report of the Public Library Inquiry* (New York: Columbia Univ. Press, 1952), p.120; Robert R. Douglass, "The Personality of the Librarian" (Ph.D. dissertation, Univ. of Chicago, 1957), p.64. (Microfilm)

[2] Donald W. Robinson, *Analysis of Motives for the Choice of a Teaching Career* (Philadelphia: Univ. of Pennsylvania, 1944), p.16, 64.

[3] Lawrence H. Stewart, "Certain Factors Related to the Occupational Choices of Experienced Teachers," *Peabody Journal of Education*, 33:235-39 (Jan. 1956).

[4] Harry C. Bauer, "Who Wants To Be a Librarian?" *ALA Bulletin*, 50:627-28 (Nov. 1956).

[5] Informal note from Professor James C. Stone, School of Education, University of California, Berkeley.

[6] Ruth E. Eckert, John E. Stecklein, and Bradley Sagan, "College Faculty Members View Their Jobs," *AAUP Bulletin*, 45:515 (Dec. 1959).

[7] Robert R. Douglass, *op. cit.*, p.64; Alice I. Bryan, *op. cit.*, p.118-19.

[8] J. Periam Danton and LeRoy C. Merritt, "Characteristics of the Gradu-

ates of the University of California School of Librarianship" (Univ. of Illinois Library School, "Occasional Papers," No.22, June 1951. Mimeographed), p.10.

[9] Albert J. Abrams, "Barriers to the Employment of Older Workers," *Annals of the American Academy of Political and Social Science*, 279:64 (Jan. 1953).

[10] Agnes L. Reagan, *A Study of Factors Influencing College Students To Become Librarians* ("ACRL Monograph," No.21 [Chicago: Assn. of College and Research Libraries, American Library Assn., 1958]), p.33.

[11] *Ibid.*, p.34-52, 95.

[12] In the special library field this advice has even been included in a recruiting manual. cf. Algene Parsons, *Using Your Subject Major as a Special Librarian* (Pasadena, Calif.: Western Personnel Institute, 1959), p.6.

[13] cf. Carl W. Hintz, "Personnel Administration—Discrimination, Despotism, Democracy," *PNLA Quarterly*, 16:18 (Oct. 1951). (A report to the Association of the results of questionnaire by the Committee on Personnel Administration). cf. also John F. Harvey, "Apply, If Thy Name Be Woman," *Library Journal*, 84:1712-13 (June 1, 1959).

[14] Morris Rosenberg, *Occupations and Values* (Glencoe, Ill.: Free Press, 1957), p.35.

[15] Theodore Caplow, *The Sociology of Work* (Minneapolis: Univ. of Minnesota Press, 1954), p.234.

[16] Morris Rosenberg, *op. cit.*, p.25 ff.

[17] *Ibid.*, p.35.

[18] Association of American Library Schools, Committee on Recruiting Personnel, "Why Library School Students Chose the Library Profession," 1953, p.20. (Mimeographed)

[19] Robert K. Merton, George G. Reader and Patricia L. Kendall, eds., *The Student-Physician: Introductory Studies in the Sociology of Medical Education* (Cambridge, Mass.: For the Commonwealth Fund by Harvard Univ. Press, 1957), p.287-93.

[20] Natalie Rogoff, "The Decision To Study Medicine," *ibid.*, p.115.

[21] Wagner Thielens, "Some Comparisons of Entrants to Medical and Law Schools," *ibid.*, p.132.

[22] Milton Wittman, *Scholarship Aid in Social Work Education* (New York: Council on Social Work Education, 1956), p.25; Herbert Bisno, *The Place of the Undergraduate Curriculum in Social Work Education*, A Project Report of the Curriculum Study, Vol. 2 (New York: Council on Social Work Education, 1959), p.82-89.

[23] Ruth E. Eckert, John E. Stecklein, and Bradley Sagan, *op. cit.*, p.515.

[24] Herbert Bisno, *op. cit.*, p.89.

[25] *Ibid.*, p.84-86.

[26] U.S. President's Commission on Higher Education, *Higher Education for American Democracy*, Vol. 1: *Establishing the Goals* (New York: Harper, 1947), p.61-65.

[27] "Discussion," in Lester Asheim, ed., *A Forum on the Public Library Inquiry* (New York: Columbia Univ. Press, 1950), p.110.

[28] *Ibid.*

[29] John F. Harvey, *Action Manual for Library Recruiters* (reprinted from *Wilson Library Bulletin*, Vol. 31 [Sept. 1956]), p.6.

[30] Theodore Caplow and Reece J. McGee, The *Academic Marketplace* (New York: Basic Books, 1958), p.109-15.

[31] "Formal placement activities... though an important factor in the development of good librarians, is perhaps not so large in importance as it may

seem during the current shortage of personnel."—Ralph Blasingame, Jr., "Placement," *Library Trends,* 3:23 (July 1954).

[32] Lloyd P. Williams, "The Pariah Status of the Teacher," *Education,* 74:261-63 (Dec. 1953).

[33] cf. Arthur J. Dibden, "Faculty, People and College Power," *AAUP Bulletin,* 40:529-36 (Dec. 1959).

[34] There are legal problems, as well as apathy, involved in this matter; see Rezia Gaunt, "Placement—To Be or Not To Be," *ALA Bulletin,* 48:84-88 (Feb. 1954).

[35] E. W. McDiarmid, "Place of Experience in Developing College and University Librarians," *Library Quarterly,* 12:614 (July 1942).

[36] John F. Harvey, *The Librarian's Career: A Study of Mobility* ("ACRL Microcard Series," No.85 [Rochester, N.Y.: Univ. of Rochester Press for the Assn. of College and Reference Libraries, 1957]), p.132, 136. Cited hereafter as *The Librarian's Career.*

[37] ——— "Variety in the Experience of Chief Librarians," *College and Research Libraries,* 19:110 (March 1958).

[38] ——— *The Librarian's Career,* p.174.

[39] ——— "Variety in the Experience of Chief Librarians," *College and Research Libraries,* 19:110 (March 1958).

[40] "Fie, If Thy Name Be Woman," *Library Journal,* 84:556 (Feb. 15, 1959).

[41] E. W. McDiarmid, *loc. cit.*

[42] Seymour M. Lipset and Reinhard Bendix, *Social Mobility in Industrial Society* (Berkeley and Los Angeles: Univ. of California Press, 1959), p.244-45.

[43] "One fifth of the librarians reported that they had paid no dues for personal memberships in library organizations in 1947."—Alice I. Bryan, *op. cit.,* p.138. It should be pointed out, however, that the Inquiry sample includes more librarians classified as "sub-professional" than does that of the present study.

[44] *Ibid.*

[45] *Ibid.,* p.52.

[46] John C. Scott, "Membership and Participation in Voluntary Associations," *American Sociological Review,* 22:321 (June 1957).

[47] National Education Association, Educational Policies Commission, *Professional Organizations in American Education* (Washington, D.C.: National Education Assn., 1957), p.12.

[48] Seymour M. Lipset, Martin A. Trow, and James S. Coleman, *Union Democracy: The Internal Politics of the International Typographical Union* (Glencoe, Ill.: Free Press, 1956), p.73-82; 410-12.

[49] George Devereux and Florence R. Weiner, "The Occupational Status of Nurses," *American Sociological Review,* 15:628-34 (Oct. 1950).

[50] John C. Scott, *op. cit.,* p.325.

[51] Mirra Komarovsky, "The Voluntary Associations of Urban Dwellers," in Logan Wilson and William L. Kolb, eds., *Sociological Analysis* (New York: Harcourt, 1949), p.378; Howard E. Freeman, Edwin Novak, and Leo G. Reeder, "Correlates of Membership in Voluntary Associations," *American Sociological Review,* 22:528-33 (Oct. 1957).

[52] Alice I. Bryan, *op. cit.,* p.140.

[53] *Ibid.,* p.441.

[54] A. B. Carson, *The Public Accounting Profession in California* (Los Angeles: Bureau of Business and Economic Research, Univ. of California, 1958), p.242-57, 282-87.

[55] Benjamin E. Powell, "A Help and Ornament Thereunto," *ALA Bulletin*, 53:685-88, 722 (Sept. 1959).
[56] Seymour M. Lipset, Martin A. Trow, and James S. Coleman, *op. cit.*, p.3-7, 412.
[57] The quotations in this paragraph are all *ibid.*, p.415-16.
[58] See, e.g., Logan Wilson, *The Academic Man* (New York: Oxford Univ. Press, 1942), p.94-95; Theodore Caplow and Reece J. McGee, *op. cit.*, p.82-85.
[59] John F. Harvey, *The Librarian's Career*, p.128.
[60] Theodore Caplow and Reece J. McGee, *op. cit.*, p.111-12.
[61] *Ibid.*, p.82. However, Eckert and her associates found that in most Minnesota undergraduate colleges, "research is considered the 'dessert' rather than the 'main course' in the life of a teacher" and that "the decision of numbers of persons to join college faculties" is based on their "primary interest in teaching."—Ruth E. Eckert, John E. Stecklein, and Bradley Sagan, *op. cit.*, p.517.
[62] Results of Gallup Poll cited in Alice I. Bryan, *op. cit.*, p.133.
[63] *Ibid.*
[64] Curtis H. Threlkeld, "Problems in the Recruitment and Adjustment of Teachers," *Bulletin of the National Association of Secondary School Principals*, 32:169-75 (March 1948).
[65] Lawrence H. Stewart, *op. cit.*, p.238.
[66] Ruth E. Eckert, John E. Stecklein, and Bradley Sagan, *op. cit.*, p.527.
[67] Alice I. Bryan, *loc. cit.*
[68] Ruth W. Gregory, "Illinois Looks at Recruiting: The Results of a Questionnaire," *Illinois Libraries*, 30:184 (May 1948).
[69] Alice I. Bryan, *loc. cit.*
[70] Ruth E. Eckert, John E. Stecklein, and Bradley Sagan, *op. cit.*, p.527-28
[71] Patricia B. Knapp, "The College Librarian: Sociology of a Professional Specialization," *College and Research Libraries*, 16:66-72 (Jan. 1955).
[72] John F. Harvey, *Action Manual for Library Recruiters* (reprinted from *Wilson Library Bulletin*, Vol. 31 [Sept. 1956]), p.[4].
[73] Herbert Bisno, *op. cit.*, p.74-76.
[74] Curtis H. Threlkeld, *op. cit.*, p.172.
[75] Morris Rosenberg, *op. cit.*, p.225.
[76] Herbert Bisno, *op. cit.*, p.70-76.
[77] Lesley M. Heathcote, "More on Middle-Level Training," *Library Journal*, 84:2106 (July 1959).
[78] Ruth E. Eckert, John E. Stecklein, and Bradley Sagan, *op. cit.*, p.525.
[79] *Ibid.*
[80] Lowest average salary among seven Minnesota institutions was $6115 in 1958-59. Estimated mean salary of the control group of academic librarians is $5600. For Minnesota teachers' salaries see "Academic Salaries, 1958-59: Report of Committee on the Economic Status of the Profession," *AAUP Bulletin*, 45:184 (June 1959).
[81] Seymour M. Lipset and Martin Trow, "Reference Group Theory and Trade Union Policy," in Mirra Komarovsky, ed., *Common Frontiers of the Social Sciences* (Glencoe, Ill.: Free Press, 1959), p.394.
[82] Robert K. Merton and Alice Kitt quoted *ibid*. Italics are Lipset and Trow's.
[83] This charge is denied by the AAUP: cf. "Academic Salaries, 1958-59: Report of Committee Z on the Economic Status of the Profession," *AAUP Bulletin*, 45:174 (June 1959).
[84] Patricia B. Knapp, *op. cit.*, p.72.
[85] Curtis H. Threlkeld, *op. cit.*, p.171.

CHAPTER V

Psychological Characteristics

In previous chapters the social origins and educational attainments of people attracted to academic librarianship were noted, a few of the things they have done since entering it analyzed, and their reactions to their experience considered. The task here is to see what kind of people this combination of selection and experience has produced. Inferences concerning this were drawn from self-perception data, i.e., from how the subjects see themselves.

The aim here is to describe the characteristics of the groups studied. Whether psychological tests should be used in the selection of candidates for entry into the profession is another question. Some writers feel that even if extremely specific and reliable measures of personality existed, their use in personnel selection would constitute an immoral invasion of privacy. The focus here is on psychological description of the group and not on individual test scores.[1]

SELF-DESCRIPTION INVENTORY

The instrument used to secure an estimate of the psychological characteristics of this group of academic librarians was the "Self-Description Inventory" developed by Edwin E. Ghiselli and his associates at the University of California, Berkeley. It is a forced-choice, adjective checklist, the subject being faced with pairs of adjectives that "are quite similar in terms of the social desirability of the traits they symbolize."[2] In the first section, the subject is asked to check the adjectives which best describe him. In the second, he is required to check those which he believes least describe him. Subjects were required to make a choice even when in doubt.

The inventory was calibrated by observing how a sample of subjects, selected so as to represent the working population of the United States, marked the lists.[3] People known to have certain traits were found to mark certain adjectives more frequently than those who were judged not to be strong in that trait. For example, highly rated supervisors see themselves as "energetic," whereas those not so highly rated tend to choose the word "ambitious." The traits were defined in terms of a person's reactions to his work rather than in relation to his general adjustment to society. (Most other personality inventories, including those used by Bryan and Douglass in studying librarians, are based on the latter approach.)

If the present study does nothing else, it gives further support to Ghiselli's finding that a forced-choice checklist is not only reliable,[4] but also at least as valid in distinguishing the "successful" from the "ordinary" as the more-elaborate instruments frequently used for this purpose. However, in this, as in other personality tests, there are many deviations from the norm.

Table 33 shows how the academic librarians in this study compare with a cross section of the general population in the traits for which the Ghiselli inventory has been calibrated. Table 34 gives these data in terms of mean scores and with more technical detail. The traits measured are defined by Ghiselli as follows:

Intelligence

The purpose of the intelligence scale is to provide an indication of general ability level. Since the items of the *Self-Description Inventory* do not involve either the usual problem

TABLE 33.
MEAN SCORES ON GHISELLI SELF-DESCRIPTION INVENTORY
EXPRESSED AS PERCENTILES OF THE ADULT
EMPLOYED POPULATION

Trait	Major Executives (224)	Minor Executives (224)	Others (228)	All (676)
Intelligence	75	76	75	76
Supervisory qualities	54	52	50	52
Initiative	49	42	36	41
Self-assurance	69	65	57	64
Occupational level	75	71	65	70

TABLE 34.
PERSONALITY TRAITS: MEAN SCORES ON THE GHISELLI SELF-DESCRIPTION INVENTORY*

Mean Scores and Standard Deviations

Trait Scored	Major Executives (224)	Minor Executives (224)	Others (228)	All (676)	Cross Section of General Nonlibrarian Population (300)
Intelligence	42.7	43.0	43.0	43.0	37.0§
	6.7	6.7	6.6	6.7	7.8
Supervisory qualities	28.4	27.9	27.6	28.0	27.0//
	5.8	6.1	6.5	6.2	6.5
Initiative†	29.6	28.5	27.2	28.4	28.6
	7.5	7.1	7.0	7.3	6.7
Self-assurance‡	27.1	26.6	25.7	26.5	24.4§
	5.7	5.8	5.9	5.7	4.8
Occupational level†	40.2	39.2	37.4	39.0	33.1§
	8.1	7.8	8.0	8.1	9.9
Decision-making power	17.8	17.3	16.9	17.3	-
	4.9	4.4	4.6	4.6	-

*Significance of difference among groups of librarians (F-test):
†.01 level
‡.05 level
Significance of difference between totals for academic librarians and cross section of general population (by T-test):
§ .01 level
// .05 level.
(T-test is the standard method of evaluating the statistical significance between two means; the F-test, or variance ratio, does essentially the same thing for three or more means.)

solving or information items in intelligence, the intelligence scale can be considered as a non-intellectual index of ability.

Supervisory Qualities

...The intent of this scale is to measure those aspects of leadership that involve direct supervision of the activities of subordinates.

Initiative

For a variety of different occupations persons are needed

needed who can act independently, and are self-sufficient to such a degree that they do not need stimulation from others in carrying out their functions. By their initiative the quality of work of such people is superior as a result of greater activity on their part and by their development of novel approaches to old problems. Their independence frees their superiors from constantly prodding them and from detailing possible courses of action. The intent of the initiative scale is to measure these qualities.

Self Assurance

Some persons attack their problems with a substantial measure of confidence, whereas others hesitate and are irresolute. The former perceive themselves as being sound in judgment, quick in adapting to new and difficult circumstances, and accurate in work methods, whereas the latter think of themselves as generally performing poorly, making many mistakes, and being inadequate in handling the problems with which they are confronted. The self-assurance scale is designed to measure the manner in which the individual perceives himself to stand on this continuum of confidence.

Occupational Level

It has been demonstrated numerous times that individuals employed in jobs at different levels in the occupational scale from professional and management personnel to unskilled workers possess different psychological characteristics. It is possible, therefore, to place an individual at a particular level on the occupational scale by matching his traits with those of individuals typically found at different levels. The purpose of the Occupational level scale is to measure these characteristics through the individual's perceptions of his characteristics.[5]

A sixth scale (scores shown in Table 34 only) refers to "decision-making power."[6] It attempts to measure qualities that differentiate between top management personnel and middle managers. These are the attributes required of the policy-maker, or as Selznick puts it, the "distinction between 'routine' and 'critical' decision-making."[7] Of men who are successful in positions calling for decision-making power, Ghiselli says:

> Theirs is a thinking role—dreaming up new ideas, looking for new fields to enter, thinking of new ways to do things. These are action-oriented men, individuals who like to be on top because they can run things the way they like and think best.[8]

Unfortunately, normative data are lacking for this scale.

EVALUATION OF RESPONSES

How academic librarians stand in the aforementioned traits will now be considered: That the intelligence scores of the subjects should be high is not surprising. It is virtually impossible for a group of people to have passed as many educational hurdles as this one has without possessing considerable intellectual ability. This finding adds a substantial bit of validation data for Ghiselli's inventory. Nor is it surprising that intelligence does not distinguish one level of the hierarchy of academic librarianship from another. This parallels the findings of Wilson[9] and of Danton and Merritt[10] that grades in college are poor predictors of success in library school or in the profession. Intellectual ability being abundant among librarians, other, scarcer qualities become critical in determining the likelihood of a person's rising in the ranks of the profession.

Attributes found among successful supervisors in other walks of life are not as common among academic librarians as one might wish. The group studied here ranks at the median of employed people generally and only at the thirtieth percentile of office supervisors in the business world. For validation of this finding, one has only to turn to the material presented in Chapter IV where it was shown that relatively few librarians find work with personnel and staff problems a major source of satisfaction and that many (20 percent of the two executive groups) find it the thing they like least about librarianship. That the minor executives should lack these qualities is particularly discouraging, for these are the direct supervisors. (The group was selected on the basis of a supervisory index!)

This poor showing on the supervisory-qualities scale has a bearing on the matter of recruitment. It was seen in Chapter IV that having worked in a library was, for many subjects, an important ingredient in the decision to become a librarian. If, then, the current complement of academic librarians are poorly qualified as supervisors and find personnel work distasteful, the effect on student assistants who are considering librarianship as a possible career must be unfortunate.

This distaste for, and lack of aptitude in, personnel supervision partially explains the strong desire among many practicing librarians that library schools deliver to them new people fully trained in specific techniques. All of this would seem to add force to Winslow's plea for more systematic on-the-job training programs, for example, sending "the new assistant to a few selected supervisors for initial training."[11] However, she also raises a difficult question:

Can we give more attention to supervisory qualities in the selection of supervisors and at the same time devise avenues of promotion for the staff member whose work merits recognition but who lacks aptitudes necessary for supervision?[12]

The subjects made an even poorer showing on the initiative scale than on the one for supervisory qualities. They rank with skilled workers in industry, i.e., with people whose work seldom requires them to solve problems on their own. This unwillingness to launch out in new directions has been seen earlier in a resistance to the "half-baked" ideas of "bright young men" and in a lack of militant concern over salary and status. This also sheds some light on the matter of professional people performing nonprofessional duties. Those lacking initiative wish to avoid risks, and there is always an element of risk in delegating important but repetitive duties to clerical workers who do not have a great deal of training or experience.

However, the pattern of scores on the initiative scale is different from that for supervisory qualities. To a statistically significant extent, initiative and degree of responsibility carried by academic librarians tend to be positively correlated. (This was not the case with the supervisory-qualities scale.) To be sure, even the major-executive group, on the average, is not very strong in initiative as compared to others on a similar occupational level. However, their average scores are better than those of the nonexecutives, and this is as it should be, or, at least, as one would expect it to be.

Thus, it would appear that much depends upon the minority of academic librarians who are receptive to change and who actively seek to improve the effectiveness of libraries. On the other hand, the oligarchical tendencies noted in Chapter IV may well continue unless ways can be found to arouse people who are by nature or nurture rather passive in their approach to the *status quo*. Perhaps a veneration for traditional values is a necessary mark of the librarian. As Grasberger points out, although "the days of the librarian's quiet, contemplative existence are gone, it must be possible to combine the demands of organization with the preservation of ... professional ideals."[13]

Academic librarians tend to be more sure of themselves than are members of the general working population. In terms of their perceptions of themselves, they resemble a criterion group whose members considered themselves to be well adjusted "to problems in every day life, especially occupational adjustment."[14]

On qualities related to self-confidence, Douglass' findings[15] lie midway between Bryan's (that public librarians tend to suffer from feelings of insecurity and inferiority)[16] and those of the present study (that academic librarians are relatively sure of themselves). Significantly, Douglass' library science student group contained people destined for both types of library work. Hence its middle position. Douglass feels that self-sufficiency is a part of a system for channeling off anxiety. Apparently the system works, for Douglass did not find neophyte librarians either unduly anxious or neurotic.[17] Nor is there any evidence of undue status anxiety or other neurotic tendencies among academic librarians. Although perhaps somewhat isolated socially, the academic librarian is protected from many sources of anxiety experienced by his colleagues in public librarianship, "a rather new and struggling profession" operating in a political setting.[18]

This pattern of self-assurance may not be entirely flattering to academic librarians. A poor showing on initiative and a strong one on self-assurance may add up to a total picture of unwarranted self-satisfaction. However, their relatively high scores on the self-assurance scale would indicate that academic librarians are well adjusted to their working environment. They do not see themselves as timid souls or as persons chronically dissatisfied with their lot in life.

The occupational-level scores of the subjects are similar to those of people in occupations at about the level of middle managers in industry and of other *salaried* professional people,[19] but lower than those of top management personnel in the business world. The following tabulation indicates how the median scores for the three groups of academic librarians compare with those for other occupational groups studied by Ghiselli:

Top management personnel	44.8
Professional personnel	44.8
Academic librarians (major-executive group)	41.7
Middle management personnel	40.9
Academic librarians (minor-executive group)	40.5
Academic librarians (non-executive group)	38.4
Clerical workers	33.5
Foremen	33.1
Skilled workers	30.1
Semiskilled workers	27.1
Unskilled workers	24.3

It is interesting to note that the largest difference among the librarians is between the middle group (minor executives) and the nonexecutives. It would appear that some of the nonexecutive librarians tend to see themselves in ways that are typical of white-collar clerical workers rather than of professional or managerial personnel. This is not surprising since, by their own testimony, many of them are doing a considerable amount of work at the clerical level. However, in the main, even the nonexecutives have a view of life and of their role in it that is essentially upper class, in contrast to the lower-middle class values Warner and his associates found to be characteristic of public school teachers.[20] The librarians lack the strong drive for advancement and the status anxiety associated with membership in the middle class of society.[21]

Academic librarians are not strong in the leadership qualities required of those who make crucial decisions in the higher echelons of government or business. Of the total possible score on "decision-making power," the average academic librarian receives a mark of only 53 percent, the lowest of all his scores on the traits measured. Nor was this unexpected. Some of the top executives in the larger libraries may make the kind of decisions this scale purports to measure, but it seems reasonable to argue that even the head librarians of most institutions play the role of middle manager. Most of their major decisions are reviewed by higher authority. Significantly, one subject who had been serving temporarily as a high-level academic administrator testified that he was very glad to resume his post as librarian.

Table 35 shows that, in general, male librarians in the control group do not score as high as their female colleagues on the self-description inventory.[22] Douglass also found this among library science students.[23] Similarly, Bryan found that male, but not female, public librarians "show less than average ascendancy in social situations, greater submissiveness, and less dominant leadership qualities than the average university student," but that the men were "more relaxed than the women."[24]

On the other hand, among the academic librarians in major executive posts, the composite score on all traits is about the same for men as for women. This may indicate that, in many cases, men with dynamic personality qualities either "go up or out," i.e., they either rise in the profession or leave it for some other line of work. In contrast to the men, many women with vigorous personalities stay on in the lower ranks. Some of these women may not wish to assume responsibility and find the financial rewards of ordinary library work adequate to their needs. Others may remain at this level despite favorable personality qualifications because the paths of advancement, either in librarianship or by transfer to another occupation, are not open to women. Still another group of women may not be able to utilize their superior qualities in seeking advancement because their mobility is limited by their husbands'

TABLE 35.
SCORES ON GHISELLI SELF-DESCRIPTION INVENTORY—BY SEX

(Comparisons should not be made between the two groups
without taking account of differences in medians.)

Trait Scored	Major Executives Median Scores*	Major Executives Percent of Scores above Median Men (163)	Major Executives Percent of Scores above Median Women (61)	Control Group Median Scores*	Control Group Percent of Scores above Median Men (109)	Control Group Percent of Scores above Median Women (334)
Intelligence	43	46%	46%	43	43%	45%
Supervisory qualities	28	53	43	28	38	47
Initiative	30	52	41	28	43	51
Self-assurance	27	44	46	26	39†	48
Occupational level	41	47	44	39	43	50
Decision-making power	18	44	54	17	37‡	50

*The medians given are "raw," i.e., the score within which the hypothetical 50th percentile falls, rather than the interpolated median.
†Difference between men and women significant at .05.
‡Difference between men and women significant at .01.

locations and occupations. The pool of leadership talent among female librarians is particularly evident in the scores on "decision-making power." Since opportunity elsewhere for women with these qualities is limited, more women than men with leadership capability come into, and remain in, the ranks of the lower administrative echelons of the profession.

Table 36 shows the relationship between occupational-level scores on the inventory and salary received. It indicates clearly that those in positions of the highest responsibility in the profession see themselves as possessing rather different characteristics from those in lesser positions. Having the personality qualities appropriate to work on the managerial level may sometimes make the head librarian seem to lack rapport with his staff. However, there is evidence that persons in authority should be somewhat detached from the rank and file.[25]

The pattern of standard deviations of test scores shown in Table 34 is interesting because of its failure to support the hypothesis that librarianship is a closely knit subculture in society. Merton, Hughes, and other social psychologists imply that physicians, and, indeed, many occupational groups of less prestige, are

TABLE 36.
OCCUPATIONAL LEVEL SCORES ON GHISELLI INVENTORY
RELATED TO SALARY*

(Relationship between personality score and salary, both groups, is almost identical when sexes are considered separately.)

Personality Inventory Score	Major Executives			Control Group		
	Less than $8000 (102)	$8000 or More (122)	Total (224)	Less than $6000 (280)	$6000 or More (165)	Total (445)
Relatively low	56%†	36%	45%	53%	50%	52%
Relatively high	44	64	55	47	50	48

*Information lacking for 38 subjects.
†Difference significant at .01 level.

relatively homogeneous in self-perception,[26] but the evidence in Table 34 supports this contention applied to librarians weakly, if at all. In some traits, such as occupational level, the process of selection and acculturation has resulted in standard deviations in self-perception scores somewhat smaller than those for a cross section of the general population. However, even in this case, the deviations from the central tendency are large. In the initiative and self-assurance traits the deviation coefficients of the academic library groups are larger than those for the general population.

Although the personality scores of the average academic librarian differ considerably from those of people engaged in other occupations, this average is a central tendency composed of a wide range of scores. Librarians fit no stereotype nor do they have an "occupational personality" in common. This finding is in agreement with those of Bryan and Douglass: Heterogeneity rather than homogeneity is characteristic of librarianship.[27] The results here parallel Douglass' finding that librarianship "does exercise a selective influence in recruiting its members," that it tends to attract people strong in certain aspects and weaker in others, but that it also attracts many who depart from the central tendencies.[28]

Just as the educational institutions they serve deal with a wide spectrum of subject matter and diverse types of students, so academic librarianship can find places for many kinds of personalities in its ranks. This may not be peculiar to librarianship. Other studies have shown that even among highly placed people in industry, many different approaches to life are found and are effective.[29] The kind of "socialization" process through which, according to Merton and his associates, the neophyte doctor goes may tend to build solidarity in that profession. On the other hand, perhaps librarianship, and even medicine, for that matter, demands flexibility and the ability to serve many different kinds of needs and to perform many different roles. At any rate, librarians have long resisted attempts to "type" them and probably will continue to do so.

Given the desirability of a variety of personality characteristics in a profession, the nature and distribution of these variations is equally crucial. The evidence here confirms that of previous studies and indicates that the overall, composite "personality profile" of academic librarianship is something less than ideally suited to the task of carrying out the complex and difficult mission of the modern academic library. If one could draw an optimum personality profile for an ideal academic library profession, the central tendencies in the more dynamic qualities would be higher. The need for imagination, ingenuity, and initiative to meet the needs of the modern college or university library program is not restricted to the office of the head librarian. Also, in the ideal academic library profession, the occupational-level scale would show a shorter tail on the clerical end of the curve. With a better division of labor and a better supply of supervisory talent, those who now, despite professional training, continue to do clerical work and to react in ways similar to other workers of this type would be replaced by people with clerical and technical, rather than professional, training.

INTERRELATIONSHIP OF PERSONALITY WITH OTHER FACTORS

For those interested in the complex but fascinating subject of multivariate analysis, four examples of the effect of combinations of personality with other factors on the career of the librarian will be discussed here. To do this economically it is necessary to introduce a summary statistical coefficient, Yule's Q.[30] This coefficient operates in a manner somewhat similar to the more familiar Pearsonian Coefficient of Correlation except that it refers to "yes or no," "high or low" attributes rather than to continuous variables. Yule's Q varies between +1.00 and -1.00 depending upon whether the association between two factors is high or low, positive or negative.

Personality and Social-Class Origin. In the case of the relationship of having a high score on the occupational-level scale of the personality inventory and holding a position as a major executive, the Q coefficient is only .14. This means that if one wished to guess whether or not a particular subject is a major executive, his ability to do so would be improved a mere 14 percent by knowing the personality score of the candidate. However, if the subjects are separated into age groups, a coefficient of .32 is found for those fifty or more years old and -.07 for those younger than fifty. There are two ways of accounting for this: First, it may be that the younger executives were chosen on the basis of formal requirements, such as advanced education, rather than of personality attributes. It may be that institutions are insisting so much on sex (male), education, and other formal qualifications that they must trust to luck that a candidate will have appropriate qualities of personality (a factor difficult to appraise, anyway). This would add substance to the complaints frequently voiced by the subjects to the effect that young, immature, and otherwise unsuitable people are rising to executive positions too frequently nowadays. The alternative explanation is that an "acculturation" phenomenon is operating here and that the "bright young men" either eventually "grow into" their roles as executives or else are removed from the executive suite before they turn fifty. Furthermore, when salary among major executives is the criterion used, personality is a more potent factor (Q = .52) among the young than among the old (Q = .20). This means that there is a large concentration of low personality scores among the young major executives earning less than $8000 a year: 66 percent of them scored below the median.

It would appear that during the post-World War II years, a bright young person with ambition, education, and, especially, a willingness to move about could become a chief librarian of a small or impecunious library without much account being taken of his personality characteristics. However, to attain major-executive status in a larger (or richer) library before age fifty required favorable personality attributes, only 38 percent of the executives in this category had scores below the median. Even so, the mature (i.e., over fifty years old) chief librarians in the highest-paying jobs tended to turn in the best scores on the personality factor, only 34 percent were below the median.

Among the minor and nonexecutives, personality bears little relationship to salary (.07), generally speaking. Among the young, it was worth a little (.13), but, among the old, virtually nothing (.01). The interesting thing here is that there is a small negative relationship between personality and age (-.14) indicating that the young made a somewhat better showing than the old. This is logical: It is to be expected that some of these younger, high-scoring librarians will secure major executive positions after they have acquired sufficient experience and perhaps more advanced education.

Personality and Social Mobility. Social psychologists have presented considerable evidence that a rapid rise on the social elevator is frequently accompanied by personality difficulties.[31] Insofar as the occupational-level scale of the Ghiselli inventory is an indicator of potential or actual maladjustment, this is seen as only a slight problem among librarians. It appears to affect the low-salaried group of major executives who have risen from lower-class family backgrounds. Of this group, 61 percent scored below the median on the occupational-level scale. Although some of the low scores are the result of an outlook on life acquired by "social inheritance," the tensions of extensive upward mobility may also be reflected here.

If it was not for the strong evidence found among other occupational groups,[32] the slight tendency among the academic librarians to exhibit adverse psychological effects of a too rapid rise in social status might not have been worth mentioning. This may be one instance in which the equivocal status of librarianship is an advantage—people from a variety of backgrounds can be accommodated without much strain. Nevertheless, the matter should be further investigated by more sensitive sociometric methods. Heads of small libraries, the ones who appear to be most affected,[33] are socially isolated on the college campus. Add to this the effects of an increasing number of people for whom entry into the profession and subsequent promotion within it represent major status shifts, and the result may be an increase in the frequency of psychological problems.

Should an increase in such problems occur, it would be obviously undemocratic and wasteful of talent to recommend that people be selected for executive positions on the basis of their fathers' social status. Rather, there is an implication here for library education, i.e., that library schools should pay considerable attention to that function of professional education which Merton, in describing the process of transforming a medical student into a doctor, calls "socialization," i.e., the acquisition of an appropriate scheme of values and set of ideals.[34]

Personality and Professional Education. Just as perplexing as the relationship between social-class origin and personality is that between type of library school attended and personality inventory scores. When the modest association (.27) between type of library school attended and achievement of high-salaried, major-executive status is, as the statisticians say, "partialled out," the relationship is found to be concentrated (Q = .56) in the group with relatively *low* personality scores. This means that attendance at a school formerly classified as Type I has the power of overcoming an unfavorable score on the inventory. This rather disturbing finding should alert the faculties of the high-prestige schools formerly classified as Type I to the power they hold as "king-makers" to the profession.

Clearly, attendance at a Type I library school, and these data refer only to the first-degree course, serves to compensate for lack of the personality attributes usually found among top managerial personnel. Perhaps this is an example of the ability of education to make effective leaders out of seemingly unpromising students. Perhaps the Type I schools have succeeded in showing such students "what leadership is" and have enabled them "to acquire certain factual information which contributes to successful leadership."[35] This training would then serve in lieu of innate qualities of leadership. However, insofar as the data reflect a tendency for librarians to be appointed to high positions on the basis of the prestige of their alma maters, it is a cause for concern.

Personality and "Variety of Experience." A final example of the interaction of two factors in a librarian's background in relation to his present status will be drawn from job mobility. Analysis not shown here has demonstrated that having a high score on the personality inventory will compensate for lack of varied experience and vice versa. The point here is that in combination the effect of both together is very great.

Following are the percentages of those scoring high on both personality and variety of experience compared to those low on both:

Major executives earning over $8000 a year who—

Scored high on personality inventory and have worked in four or more libraries	41%
Scored low in the inventory and have worked in fewer than four libraries	14%

Thus, it appears that the librarian with neither the personality attributes typical of executives nor the variety of experience that would prepare him for the role has little chance of entering the top administrative echelons of academic librarianship.[36]

In Chapter IV, reference was made to those who were described in Gray's "Elegy" as "mute inglorious Miltons," i.e., talented people who escaped fame by sticking to the country village. In this context, those with high personality scores who have not gone out and acquired experience in a variety of libraries and who, as a consequence, have remained on the lower salary levels, fall into the "inglorious Milton" category. The following percentage tabulation shows the proportions of such persons in each of the groups studied:[37]

Major executives	10%
Control subjects	20%

Although there are probably various other possible reasons for their low salaries, it would appear that up to one fifth of the control-group librarians have remained in a low salary status because they were unwilling or unable to move about and acquire the varied experience required for positions for which they have desirable personality qualifications. In the major-executive group, on the other hand, the pool of librarians with suitable personalities but without varied experience is not large.

The situation with respect to the heads of the smaller libraries (i.e., those earning between $6000 and $8000 a year in 1958) is particularly unfavorable: 34 percent of this group is below the median on both the personality and experience criteria, compared to only 14 percent of the major executives earning $8000 or more. Indications are that the smaller institutions might well pay more attention to both personality and experience in selecting chief librarians and less to such factors as the sex of the applicant and the prestige of the institution from which he holds degrees.

These few examples will give an idea of the complexity of the interaction of factors in the career of the academic librarian. No simple solution is offered to the problems faced by the individual librarian as he tries to plan the course of his career or to the selection officer as he attempts to secure the best person for a particular position. However, multivariate analysis, of which the above are only crude examples, may help both to consider the odds in favor of or against a particular course of action. This type of analysis, no matter how sophisticated, should not, and probably cannot, be expected to produce a brave new world of statistical determinism in personnel matters.

SUMMARY

As a group, academic librarians can be described as cultured and intelligent, but, like the library science students studied by Douglass, lacking in the traits "which are most closely associated with forceful leadership."[38] In one trait, self-assurance, college and university librarians appear to be stronger than librarians in other types of libraries. This may reflect the greater stability of their segment of the profession.

Those who have the scarce dynamic qualities of initiative and self-assurance tend to rise in the ranks of the profession. Both male and female librarians in major-executive positions tend to score rather well on the traits studied, but in the middle management and nonexecutive groups a greater proportion of women than of men made high scores on the more dynamic personality attributes.

It may be that many library positions do not require a great deal of initiative or originality from the incumbents. However, supervisory aptitude is very frequently required of them. The fact that many subjects scored low in this trait is a cause for concern.

In general, the subjects see themselves as possessing qualities similar to those selected by people in other occupations on a similar prestige level. The personality inventory shows them to be middle-level professional people, and this is where outside observers have also placed them.[39] However, this general picture is based on the average of a rather wide range of scores on the inventory. Many academic librarians have an outlook on life similar to that of people in clerical, rather than professional, occupations. This may reflect the fact that too many of them are actually doing work on a clerical level. As position in the hierarchy of the profession increases, the self-descriptions given by academic librarians resemble more and more those of other professional and managerial people and less and less those of clerical workers.

Multivariate analysis illustrates the complexity of the process by which a given academic librarian is produced. In some cases, education and experience tend to reinforce the effects of the psychological factors; in others, to nullify them. If nothing else, this analysis shows why attempts to find simple criteria by which librarians may be recruited and selected are doomed to failure.

NOTES

[1] William H. Whyte, *The Organization Man* (New York: Simon & Schuster, 1956), p.171-201.

[2] Edwin E. Ghiselli, "Self-Description Inventory" (Univ. of California, 1957), p.3. (Processed)

[3] *Ibid.*, p.6-7.

[4] Reliability of coefficients range from .56 to .90. All but one (Self-Assurance) are above .70. *Ibid.*, p.7.

[5] *Ibid.*, p.3-5.

[6] Scoring weights for this scale were obtained from Lyman W. Porter of the Psychology Department, University of California. Lyman W. Porter and Edwin E. Ghiselli, "The Self Perceptions of Top and Middle Management Personnel" (Univ. of California, [1957]), p.13 (Processed), discusses this scale but does not give the scoring key.

[7] Philip Selznick, *Leadership in Administration* (Evanston, Ill.: Row, Peterson, 1957), p.22.

[8] University of California, Public Information—Radio, "Who's the Boss?" ("University Explorer" Broadcast, No.1542, April 28, 1957), p.3. (Mimeographed)

[9] Eugene H. Wilson, "Pre-Professional Background of Students in a Library School," *Library Quarterly*, 8:162 (April 1938).

[10] J. Periam Danton and LeRoy C. Merritt, "Characteristics of the Graduates of the University of California School of Librarianship" (Univ. of Illinois Library School, "Occasional Papers," No.22, June 1951), p.13. (Mimeographed)

[11] Amy Winslow, "Supervision and Morale," *Library Trends*, 3:48 (July 1954).
[12] *Ibid.*
[13] Franz Grasberger, "On the Psychology of Librarianship," *Library Quarterly*, 24:38 (Jan. 1954).
[14] *Ibid.*, p.12.
[15] Robert R. Douglass, "The Personality of the Librarian" (Ph.D. dissertation, Univ. of Chicago, 1957), p.81. (Microfilm)
[16] Alice I. Bryan, *The Public Librarian: A Report of the Public Library Inquiry* (New York: Columbia Univ. Press, 1952), p.42.
[17] Robert R. Douglass, "The Personality of the Librarian" (dissertation abstract, Univ. of Chicago, 1957), p.10. (Mimeographed)
[18] Everett Hughes, "Discussion," in Lester Asheim, ed., *A Forum on the Public Library Inquiry* (New York: Columbia Univ. Press, 1950), p.107-10.
[19] The control group of librarians had a median score similar to those for nurses, analysts, personnel officers, accountants, and industrial engineers. —Edwin E. Ghiselli, "Self-Description Inventory" (Univ. of California, 1957), p.15. (Processed)
[20] W. Lloyd Warner, Robert J. Havighurst, and Martin B. Loeb, *Who Shall Be Educated?* (New York: Harper, 1944), p.171.
[21] Seymour M. Lipset and Reinhard Bendix, *Social Mobility in Industrial Society* (Berkeley and Los Angeles: Univ. of California Press, 1959), p.244-46.
[22] In Ghiselli's cross section of the general population, women tended to have higher scores than men on intelligence, supervisory qualities, and occupational level; lower on initiative and self-assurance (Edwin E. Ghiselli, "Self-Description Inventory" [Univ. of California, 1957], p.20-24. [Processed]). In the "control group" of librarians (see Table 35), a greater proportion of women than men scored high on all of the scales.
[23] Robert R. Douglass, *op. cit.* (abstract), p.7.
[24] Alice I. Bryan, *loc. cit.*
[25] V. M. Wilson, "Some Personality Characteristics of Industrial Executives." *Occupational Psychology*, 30:228-31 (Oct. 1956).
[26] Robert K. Merton, *Social Theory and Social Structure* (rev. ed.; Glencoe, Ill.: Free Press, 1957), p.368-84; Everett C. Hughes, "Personality Types and the Division of Labor," in his *Men and Their Work* (Glencoe, Ill.: Free Press, 1958), p.42-55; Mary Jean Huntington, "The Development of a Professional Self-Image," in Robert K. Merton, George G. Reader, and Patricia L. Kendall, eds., *The Student-Physician* (Cambridge, Mass.: For the Commonwealth Fund by Harvard Univ. Press, 1957), p.178-187.
[27] Robert R. Douglass, *op. cit.* (abstract), p.7; Alice I. Bryan, *op. cit.*, p.43.
[28] ——— *op. cit.* (abstract), p.7.
[29] cf. William H. Whyte, *op. cit.*, p.198.
[30] G. Udny Yule and M. G. Kendall, *An Introduction to the Theory of Statistics* (London: Charles Griffin, 1950), p.30-48. For discussions of the interpretation of Q and extensions of the principal to polytomies, see Morris Zelditch, *A Basic Course in Sociological Statistics* (New York: Holt, 1959), p.168 ff., and Leo A. Goodman and William H. Kruskal, "Measures of Association for Cross Classifications," *Journal of the American Statistical Association*, 49:732-64 (Dec. 1954), and their "Further Discussion and References," *ibid.*, 54:123-63 (March 1959).
[31] This research is summarized in Seymour M. Lipset and Reinhard Bendix, *op. cit.*, p.244-55.

[32] For a popularized summary, see Vance Packard, *The Status Seekers* (New York: McKay, 1959), p.256.

[33] This is similar to the findings of W. Lloyd Warner and James C. Abegglen that business executives suffering from too rapid a rise in social status were concentrated on the lower levels of business leadership rather than the top echelons.—*Big Business Leaders in America* (New York: Harper, 1955), p.84-107.

[34] Robert K. Merton, George G. Reader, and Patricia L. Kendall, eds., *op. cit.*, p.287-93.

[35] J. Periam Danton, *Education for Librarianship: Criticisms, Dilemmas, and Proposals* (New York: School of Library Service, Columbia Univ., 1946), p.18.

[36] cf. John F. Harvey, "Variety in the Experience of Chief Librarians," *College and Research Libraries*, 19:107-10 (March 1958).

[37] In the major executive group, low salary is defined as less than $8000; in the control group, less than $6000. Lack of varied experience, in both cases, is defined as having worked in fewer than four libraries.

[38] Robert R. Douglass, *op. cit.* (abstract), p.10.

[39] W. Lloyd Warner, Marchia Meeker, and Kenneth Eels, *Social Class in America* (Chicago: Science Research Associates, 1949), p.135. Librarians were rated as being in class 2 of a 7-point scale by Warner's informants.

CHAPTER VI

Implications of Findings

To this point, the approach has been to play the role of the descriptive scientist and present the facts of academic librarianship as it now is, and to describe the influences that have played upon academic librarians during the past fifty years or so. Projection of past trends into the future is a dangerous process, but one has no other guide to the future except the past. One of the respondents put this dilemma so well that her comments are worth reproducing in some detail. The respondent, head librarian of a small eastern university, doubts that information about the characteristics of those holding (with varying degrees of success) positions in academic libraries would necessarily have a bearing on recruiting or guidance:

> It is my guess that you will find a number of us arrived at our present state more by chance than by design, and the personnel situation in librarianship is now so far out of line that it seems unwise to base any assumption on current findings.
> The gap in information you mention is not accidental. Academic librarians are so varied a group that it will be difficult—if not impossible—to generalize about them.... The academic librarian of the future may bear no resemblance to the members of the current crop. New abilities are bound to be required, and guidance officers and educators will have to accept this fact.
> I am happy to know that someone is interested in academic librarians, for their lot is a peculiarly difficult one. Academic communities are so bound by tradition that the progressive librarian finds many obstacles in the way of effective performance. The surface of the situation has been scratched many times—

in numerous articles—but no one, to my mind, has yet arrived at the basic problems that lie well below the surface. It is true that your current efforts may not deal with these, but perhaps your interest will lead you to do something about them at a later date.

It is true that the present investigation is but a prelude to more intensive and specific studies. However, certain generalizations can be made, and certain trends may well continue. The very confirmation of several of the assumptions made in the above letter should be of help to the guidance officer. Academic librarians are indeed a "varied group." Thus, there are many places in the profession for the able maverick, but if the guidance officer is to place such a person well, he must know what the central tendencies are. That "new abilities are bound to be required" is here amply demonstrated. By comparing librarians with other groups, it has been possible to identify some of these abilities, notably, that ability to supervise other workers is sadly lacking among present academic librarians. Again, it has been shown that while librarians generally lack qualities for dealing effectively with "communities...bound by traditions," those with initiative have tended to rise in the profession and may be expected to be more in demand in the future.

That "the personnel situation in librarianship is now...far out of line" is also confirmed, and pressure that something be done about it will certainly be felt in the future. Overwhelmingly, librarians look to the library schools, rather than to their own efforts or to academic administration, for remedies for these chaotic conditions. However, leadership will come from a relatively small group, and every effort should be made by "guidance officers and educators" to pick out and encourage these rare people. Finally, this survey has attempted to probe a bit further than its predecessors and has found some "basic problems that lie well below the surface." One of these is the problem of changing social origin of librarians, a phenomenon of which most librarians are but vaguely aware.

In interpreting his findings, the writer has been greatly aided by the comments of his respondents, of which the foregoing is an example. Although the number who gave extensive comments is not great (40 percent), those who did were wonderfully articulate and capable of penetrating insights into the problems of the profession. It is on these that the following analysis of the implications of the study will be based.

Table 37 shows the topics selected by the subjects for free comment. A few comments on the distribution of topics chosen may be appropriate before examples of their content are given. Of

TABLE 37.
TOPICS CHOSEN FOR FREE COMMENT

(Responses to the question: "Do you have suggestions for improving librarianship or library education?")

Topic chosen for Comment*	Major Executives (103)	Minor Executives (97)	Others (85)	Total (285)
Admission and survival standards of library schools	18%	21%	25%	21%
Course requirements and content in library schools	47	64	46	52
Teaching standards in library schools	10	6	10	9
Degree structure and placement of library science in the curriculum of higher education	16	12	7	12
Apprentice, in-service, and sub-professional training	9	10	10	10
Professional attitudes and habits	30	25	25	27
Status of profession	9	7	12	9
Salaries and working conditions	4	6	22	10
Recruiting for librarianship	9	6	4	6
Library operating problems (other than personnel problems)	5	4	2	4
Other topics	24	35	19	26
Proportion of total number of subjects who did not offer comment	56	68	65	60

*Many subjects mentioned more than one topic (ratio is 1.8 topics per subject who mentioned any topic at all). Hence, totals add up to more than 100%.

the two general topics suggested in the question "librarianship and library education," more than half (56 percent) of the comments were on library education. Another popular item, "Professional attitudes and habits," is also related to education. It reflects the dissatisfaction of the old hands in librarianship with the library schools for not selecting and winnowing applicants more stringently. The result, according to these respondents, is that the products lack appropriate professional attitudes. The middle managers seem to be the most frequently dissatisfied with what is taught in library schools. As noted in Chapters IV and V, some of this dissatisfaction probably reflects the impatience of middle management librarians with training and supervisory duties and the lack of aptitude of many of them for this phase of their work. Hence, their desire to push this function back to the library schools.[1]

Despite the remarks made in the cover letter about the importance of this study to those concerned with the problem of recruiting new librarians, few subjects had much to say about this problem. Apparently, most respondents feel that recruiting is a function of the library schools. The finding here is quite to the contrary: It is the personal influence of older librarians that brings new ones into the profession.[2]

The last row of Table 37, "Other topics," reflects the variety of points of view held by the subjects. Variety seems to be a dominant characteristic of the profession. One of the things which seems to make the lot of the academic librarian "a particularly difficult one" is that it consists of many small problems which nobody else seems to understand or appreciate. According to Hughes, this is typical of not only middle-brow professions like librarianship, but of many other occupational groups in modern society, characterized, as it is, by extreme specialization.[3] In the sections to follow, several of the comments made by the subjects will be discussed in some detail to illustrate the findings of this report.

SOCIAL CHARACTERISTICS

One of the basic problems that "lie well below the surface" of librarianship results from the changing social backgrounds of the people entering this and other professions. The finding here is that whereas formerly membership in the profession was virtually restricted to the sons and daughters of genteel, although not always well-to-do, people, recently librarians have been coming from among the laboring or lower-middle classes. It was further noted that advanced professional, rather than academic, education has been the medium for this upward mobility and that the energy characteristic of those who break into librarianship from lower-class origins often carries them to the lower, but not the highest, executive positions. Finally, it has been shown that this tendency has psychological overtones and may create problems of adjustment. A female cataloger in a liberal arts college came the closest to recognizing this tendency when she said:

> Some librarians pride themselves on a kind of anti-intellectualism. There seems to be little to distinguish them from office workers. Even the so-called "crack" librarian too frequently falls into this class. I have known self-educated village librarians in the East who had more intellectual curiosity without a library degree, in fact without a college education, than many holding fine positions in excellent colleges and other institutions of higher learning.
>
> Schools of librarianship should, I believe, hold their students up to high professional standards and ethics. There is no doubt that librarians in general are not held in the esteem that teachers are, or doctors and lawyers. Too much emphasis is placed upon skills, tools, "know how"; too little on the accumulated wisdom of the ages. An able physics teacher, professor in a good liberal arts college, remarked to a librarian who loves learning for its own sake: "You read books. Most college librarians I know go to the movies."

What this librarian calls "anti-intellectualism" may, in many cases, be just that. Furthermore, it may stem, as Talcott Parsons suggests, from the pragmatism of the middle classes and the "Populism" of American mass society.[4] On the other hand, "anti-intellectualism" is a handy epithet that may be given to any departure from the genteel, but passive, tradition of librarianship to a more aggressive, efficient, and unsentimental approach to books. The implication is that the librarian in question has been contaminated by the pragmatism of a nether stratum of society.

The writer of the above passage also recognizes another tendency found in the survey, to wit, that it is possible to substitute educational qualifications for other background characteristics normally considered appropriate to the librarian. Sometimes this is "good," as in the case of the ability of the old second-year master's in librarianship to overcome the disadvantage of being a woman. It may be "bad" if, in the language of the social psychologist, professional education trains people in the skills of the profession but does not introduce them into an appropriate "awareness of role."[5] One of the problems here is a lack of a consensus about what the role of a librarian is. The writer of the above quotation takes a broader view of this than many: she refers to "intellectual curiosity" and a regard "for the wisdom of the ages." Other librarians wish to focus their attention entirely on the bibliophilic and esthetic values that are traditional in the profession. Still others see technical competence as a most valuable, and misunderstood, hallmark of the exemplary librarian.

In discussing the ambiguous role of the librarian, Talcott Parsons uses Emile Durkheim's word, *anomie,* which means "normlessness." This *anomie* leads the librarian to a passive, "custodial" attitude toward his function in society, whereas, according to Parsons, he "is to some degree a custodian not merely of books but of standards of excellence, and his role of being helpful can readily involve an ingredient of educating the client to better standards."[6]

Among people recruited from the lower strata of society, the image of the librarian's role is not invariably a radical one. For example, one respondent, who takes as her model the intellectual emphasis of the old aristocracy of the Atlantic seaboard, as opposed to the pragmatism of the "bright young men," is from a lower middle class, midwestern background. Her father was a self-educated small businessman who "devoted all his life to books" and "read theology." It is said that the recent convert to a religion is likely to be the most zealous in it; thus, those who are recent entrants into the segments of society where the "furniture of the mind" is highly valued may be the most concerned about the intellectual status of the profession. It is likely that these librarians will, by their energy and zeal, liberalize the profession without diluting its essential character as an intellectual pursuit.

EDUCATION FOR LIBRARIANSHIP

One of the persistent problems in educating librarians has been the dilemma of uniformity versus diversity. The discussion of "socialization" in Chapter IV pointed to the desirability of librarians' having a common store of knowledge and ideals, an "occupational personality." As a 1953 workshop on "The Core of Education for Librarianship" concluded, "if librarianship means anything as a profession, there must be basic essentials."[7] On the other hand, as the loyal opposition stated at the same conference, "librarianship is encyclopedic" and "where certain broad areas of subject matter... seem to be common to all types of library work, the approaches are so different that special orientation is required" for each type of library work.[8]

In addition to the core programs in the curriculum, one of the unifying developments of the post-World War II years has been the simplification and standardization of the degree structure. This eliminated the old-style master's degree and the undergraduate programs formerly classified as Type III. Both of these were diversifying elements. Many respondents are not happy with such attempts at unification and call for more diversity. Nor are they satisfied with the relationship between the subject-matter preparation of the librarian and his professional training.

For example, to compensate for the virtual demise of the old-style master's degree (shown here to have been particularly important to women who aspired to become middle managers or heads of smaller libraries), one male head librarian from a library school formerly classified as Type III (i.e., offering a year of library science as part of an undergraduate curriculum) has the following suggestions:

> I am concerned by the fact that present Library School programs for advanced graduate work beyond the basic professional degree are not being provided for the great bulk of academic librarians. Only a few will be able to enter Ph.D. programs and the great majority have no alternative choice now of doing further work which will broaden and deepen their interests in a particular speciality. I think the profession and library schools should consider offering a block of advanced specialized courses which would not necessarily result in a degree but perhaps a certificate or registration as a master cataloger, reference librarian, etc. Such a program would give advanced specialized work, [and] result in a profession which would have its licensed catalogers etc., and act as a spur for further study to qualify. Each of these programs might consist of about 15 hours and could be given in summer sessions on a rotating basis, perhaps, with seminar type organization or individual problems as the teaching method.

Such a program would lend status to such activities as cataloging that now do not appear attractive to neophyte librarians. It would also provide a basis for rewarding special skill and training in library work. Another librarian, this time a woman in the non-executive category, argues for advanced professional education:

> [for] the preparation of personnel who intend to enter library administration at the middle management level.... Perhaps the answer is more institutes such as the Rutger's Library School has held recently for the middle management group and top library administrators.[9]

Another suggestion is that professional training and general education be coordinated and proceed together. This, of course, implies that the decision to enter this type of work be made early. It has been shown here that persons who either make this decision during their college years or indicated that they could have been persuaded to decide then but who actually put it off tend to be successful in terms of position and salary more frequently than others. These are the ones who would benefit still further from a coordinated program of general and professional education. One female librarian said:

> I think that the library education program should be coordinated throughout the entire college program and students interested in Library Science should have more counseling during their first years of college education, and that they should take more language courses if they are interested in college library work and should have better, broader general knowledge.... I think certain definite courses should be required before the library science instruction is begun and the program should be laid out for the entire college course. The student should be given some help in reaching a decision as to what kind of library work he wants to pursue and help him in planning his course work so that he will get a good background for his library science.

Evidence was presented in Chapter IV that such a program might well attract more, as well as better, people into librarianship.

The feeling among many librarians that neophytes have not been sufficiently grounded in library skills and techniques was discussed in Chapter III. The attitude on the part of practicing librarians that new professionals should require no further training is as much an indication of lack of supervisory ability and training of the older librarians as it is a deficiency in the new librarians. It was also pointed out that this was but one aspect of the general problem of separating clerical from professional work, that what the old hands really wanted to delegate to the neophytes is not technical, but clerical, work. The new librarians do not take well to this, more through lack of interest in subprofessional work than through lack of skill or aptitude for skilled work on a professional level.

To remedy this, several subjects recommend that librarianship be divided into at least three levels, each with its appropriate level of education. Advanced education would be the instrument for moving from one level to another. This is, of course, implied in the foregoing quotations, but it is further developed in the following statements from head librarians. The first is a woman who says:

> I find graduates of the present library curriculum are

inclined to live on the theoretical plane and have not had enough training to be of practical help. Many of them seem to be lacking in accuracy and are not systematic in their work. My personal opinion is that there should be more of the training that used to be obtained in the old B.S. in L.S.—but within the 4 yr. curriculum. Then the M.S. on the theoretical and graduate level would make a more useful and better trained assistant. I realize that those skills can be obtained on the job, but with a small staff, the librarian does not have time to do all of that training and too often the new graduates seem to feel a great deal of the work that has to be done in a library is beneath them.

A male head librarian couches the same idea in more general terms:

I think the profession moved too hastily in trying to put all education for librarianship at the master's degree level or higher. I would prefer a system in which some library science would be taken at the undergraduate level, say 12 to 15 hours, to be followed by the master's or doctor's program. Some of the material which should be covered at the undergraduate level now is part of the graduate program, and weakens it. The number of librarians could be increased if we could have beginners in the profession coming to us after four years in college, then going to library school later for a master's degree after they've had some experience. We'd get better students in the library school if we did this, and could deepen and broaden the courses offered for the master's and doctor's degrees.

Finally, one head librarian, a woman, sees the answer in the presently unaccredited library schools. Furthermore, she sees in her proposal a method of reversing the trend toward an increasing proportion of men in the profession:

I am chiefly concerned about reinstating accreditation of undergraduate library schools. It seems to me that a number of such schools—really departments—in teacher's colleges are trying to become eligible for accreditation as graduate schools, under the present ALA plan, with a consequent lowering of accrediting standards at that level. They could be accredited legitimately as undergraduate schools and many students would be happy to go to accredited schools at that level,—particularly girls, who may not want graduate training until they see if they're going to marry.

This proposal may have some merit.[10] Perhaps the reason so few graduates of Type III and unaccredited curricula have come into academic librarianship is that these schools did not emphasize this type of library work. However, now that the former teachers' colleges are offering more academic emphasis in their curricula,[11] academic libraries may find library schools attached to these institutions an appropriate source of personnel for a "middle service."

Moving the "fundamentals" of library technique into undergraduate programs or into apprenticeship programs would, in the opinion of many academic librarians, leave the way clear for introducing more academic content into graduate programs. The seeking of advanced degrees, separate from library science training, is well regarded by librarians in service and is, as has been shown here, frequently rewarded in terms of salary. However, a program in library science that includes a major emphasis in some discipline, say, a behavioral or natural science, is thought by some, including the present writer, to be more efficient and less time-consuming. Behavioral or natural science is suggested in the light of the finding that large numbers of people with degrees in history and the humanities come into librarianship anyway, whereas the other kinds of specialization are relatively rare. One respondent, a subject specialist herself, after noting that "there are many positions...which require no more than the elementary courses of library science," went on to say:

> I believe subject specialization for advanced students is very highly to be desired. I think subject proficiency should be required for the M.A. By "proficiency" I mean one should be able to teach the subject in at least high school level. Library schools should encourage and stress subject specialization for candidates for the master's degree.

The rationale for this is given by another subject specialist who declares:

> ...every qualified librarian should be required to be a competent research-scholar in some field of studies (other than library science) of his own choice. A librarian who is a specialist only in library technique is like a teacher who is expert only in the methodology of teaching, is a sub-standard person who will never gain public respect nor would he deserve it.

There is danger in this proposal if it were to be carried to the point where librarians become no longer librarians, but second-class—and frustrated—sociologists, biologists, and historians.

However, familiarity with the processes of scholarship comes only with having engaged in them, and such familiarity is important to most university librarians on any level above the quasi-clerical. An interdisciplinary approach to this is probably better than that advocated in the quotation above, but the bureaucratic structure of universities makes such interdepartmental efforts difficult. Nevertheless, the Graduate Library School at the University of Chicago probably gained much of its great prestige by virtue of being able to relate librarianship to other disciplines.[12] The doctoral program in library science at the University of Michigan also involves intensive work in a field other than library science.[13]

Despite the many, sometimes conflicting, criticisms levied at the general and, especially, the professional education of librarians, both the direct testimony of the librarians and the impersonal evidence from coefficients of association indicate that educational attainment is the factor by which librarians (and those who appoint them) put the most store. As one subject summed up the matter:

> ...library education needs to be more practical, ideally achieved by an internship program. It also needs to be more intellectual, to be achieved by graduate work in subject fields. ...Present library training seems to be a reasonably satisfactory compromise among these needs.

Suggestions for reform are directed toward improving this compromise, and few who consider librarianship to be a profession with a distinctive mission question the importance of specialized education for it. If nothing else, this survey has provided facts and figures to substantiate the importance of both general and professional education for a so-called profession in transition.[14] The task ahead is to bring the two into closer and more efficient relationship.[15]

CAREER FACTORS

Throughout this survey, one gathers the impression that librarians in service tend to put all of the responsibility for present problems of the profession, and to pin all of their hopes for improved conditions in the future, on the library schools. The facts and figures presented show, however, that while professional education is an important ingredient in the present accomplishments and failures of the profession, many other factors have influenced the careers of today's academic librarian. Although the power of education to modify these other factors has been shown to be great, library education tends to follow the leadership of the profession as well as to supply those leaders. The relatively few comments of those who chose to talk about subjects other than the content of library education are worthy of particular notice.

It has been shown in Chapter IV that the recent leaders of the profession tend to have come from among those who became interested in librarianship relatively early in life. A valuable place can be found in the ranks for those who enter late, and many leaders are also recruited from this source, but the chances of winning creative minds are best if an occupation selects its recruits from among college students rather than waiting for them to drift into it later in life. Perhaps because so many of them are late entrants themselves, few of the subjects cared to comment on this factor. Perhaps, also, they may have felt that its importance was self-evident. One reference librarian, a woman of mature years, who did recognize the importance of early recruitment and selection of candidates, put it this way:

> Begin with high school assemblies and explain width of library jobs. Don't let them "fall in" after failure in other fields— discover librarianship as a semi-failure field.... Begin library reference and content courses in under-grad years to (1) give benefit of knowledge of tools as student goes along.... (2) Meet competition of other graduate fields who [sic] get themselves before the student early and insidiously.

Librarians, generally, are wary of "recruiting" if this means accepting marginal people. They are aware that one of the time-honored ways an occupation becomes a profession is by restricting access to those who meet the qualifications and master the art. Catalogers are particularly frank about this. One put it quite candidly by saying:

> Library schools should ask for a *good scholastic* background (besides all the other things that may make good librarians) and implant in their students the wish to be considered on equal footing with other members of professional groups. There is no question that many people without library school could become good librarians but libraries should adhere to similar practices as hospitals or law courts etc. and ask these people to comply with the rules set up for becoming a librarian.

She indicates further that if university libraries are to adhere to these standards, they have the corresponding obligation to give scholarships and also "'time' to promising aspirants—that in the end all professional librarians should have a truly professional background." Only a few go so far as to suggest that the government regulate the conditions of entrance into professional work, but one cataloger declared:

> The library professional organizations should emphasize certification on a national level. National boards of education for librarianship should emphasize and enforce standards for entering the profession.

However, proposals for certification that the Public Library Inquiry made for public libraries[16] would find little favor among academic librarians generally. Apparently, the academic people feel that their segment of the profession is sufficiently unified to enforce standards, with, of course, the help of the library schools.

The evidence here confirms that of Harvey in showing the importance of experience as an ingredient in the career of the head librarian.[17] However, head librarians in 1958 tended to have had more varied experience than those studied earlier by Harvey. Several respondents commented on the importance of experience and made references to the appointment of inexperienced young men to responsible positions. One head librarian felt that experience should be the chief factor in success as an administrator:

> Library administration cannot be taught in library schools. There is nothing like on-the-job-experience, yet graduates of library schools want to start out as departmental heads or head librarians. I was considered a professional librarian for 15 years before attending a library school. I learned nothing in that school that I did not know from experience. I went to a library school solely to obtain the union card necessary for advancement (or even appointment) in a college library.

This is an extreme position and is in contrast to that of the subjects quoted in the paragraphs immediately preceding who regard the "union card" function of professional library education as of primary importance in maintaining and enhancing the status of the profession. The more usual reaction is to place the responsibility on the library schools for this and for most other problems of the profession. Said one head of a technical processes unit:

> Students should be impressed with the need to start somewhere besides the top unless they have considerable experience in the field. Some schools have gotten too far away from the old-time practise work in reference and cataloging; it shows on the job. The schools should do something to reduce the number of

individuals accepting administrative positions too soon after graduation; they can not command the respect of a well-trained staff. Too often staff members have to spend their time educating the "boss," instead of being able to depend on him or her to lead.

Not only should library schools, in the opinion of some respondents, use their power as personnel placement agencies to enforce standards of experience, but they should also provide practical experience as part of the curriculum. Again a cataloger speaks:

Library education should give students more actual practice in interior workings of the library such as *actual,* not hypothetical, problems in cataloging and bindery and mending methods. Nothing can replace actual experience in such cases and the only way to obtain it is either working while attending school or instituting some sort of workshop-type plan.

Some go so far as to tear a page directly from the medical-education book. As one would expect, the following comes from a medical librarian:

[Librarians should have] supervised training as part of library school (non-credit) for M.S. Degree. Internship 1 year after M.S. Residency 1 year after DLS.

It will be noted that it is the catalogers and other technical process people who take up the cudgels for the role of experience in preserving and transmitting the "intellectually based technique" of which they consider themselves the guardians. Although it has been shown in the foregoing pages that library leadership probably requires quite different personality characteristics from those required of practitioners of the art itself, woe unto the leader who has not had contact with the actual work a librarian does!

The exaggerated importance attached to experience by those who entered the profession by that route serves to point up the reasons why varied experience is of inestimable worth to an administrator. Again a technical processes chief (female) speaks:

This may, coming from one with no library school degree, sound like sour grapes, but is the result of almost thirty years of working with all kinds of librarians, being supervised and supervising. Recent library school education has taken the fun out of being a librarian. It instills class distinction—"this is clerical, therefore I must not do it," it develops would-be-administrators without experience or knowledge of the many routines which go into the successful management of a department or library. Every real profession—teach [ing], law, medicine—has an apprenticeship but librarians think that two weeks visiting libraries in the spring of the graduate year is sufficient on the job training. Inability to complete successful training in all routines from filing to giving Mrs. Housewife and Professor Erudite the help they need at their own level, would disqualify one from becoming a librarian even more than failing to pass a course in the history of printing. Thorough knowledge of the interdependence of every department to make an efficiently functioning library is essential. No prima donnas needed. Librarianship is a practical, commonsense science. Why not work to make it so?

Of course, one of the functions of professional education is to modify attitudes such as this by showing that administration is itself a technique, if not a science, and that a broad understanding of the functions of each department of the library can be taught more effectively in school than through experience in mending books. Life is too short for the administrator to have practiced all of the arts he may have under his supervision. Nevertheless, even if the professional administrator does, as one respondent indicated, "understand the interdependency of every department," it will do him little good if his staff does not believe it. And they may not, unless he can show evidence of having had some practical experience in at least a few of the departments somewhere at some time.

Quantitative data in this survey on variety of experience were limited to the number of libraries in which subjects have worked. However, these data do strongly suggest that head librarians recently have been more adequately grounded in experience than they were during the pre-World War II period studied by Harvey and referred to by the cataloger who wrote the following indictment:

When I was in school at Columbia U—, so many of the young (men in particular) were preparing to become administrators from studying. They were encouraged in this attitude in their course. Since than I have discovered that thru inexperience they commit "faux pas" in business dealings which could have been avoided thru experience with an older or well-trained librarian as supervisor. Perhaps this has been remedied by now.

Apparently it has, for, in general, the young in academic librarianship have tended to move about more frequently than the old. Furthermore, mobility of this sort has been rewarded more frequently among the young than among the old. However, this may be bad news for those who wish to sink roots in a community or an institution and grow with it by promotion from within. It should also be noted that increasing recognition of the importance of experience does not imply that one should not prepare to become an administrator "from studying." Advanced education continues to be richly rewarded by advancement in position and salary.

If length, as well as variety, of experience is important in preparing a librarian for positions of responsibility, the situation is less optimistic. Length of experience as reflected in the age of librarians at the time of the survey is virtually unrelated to salary. It may well be that education and variety of experience, together with the emphasis on youth in our culture generally, are such strong influences that length of service has been crowded out as a criterion for advancement. The bitterness of the following woman, again a cataloger, may not be entirely unjustified:

> Might the library profession do well to establish an attitude or policy in regard to librarians who have rendered long years of service and who have much to offer in the way of understanding and experience? There is a strong tendency for a new head librarian to be so involved in material accomplishments and visible progress, that he does not give thoughtful consideration to this matter. Consequently the creative and interesting is held up to tempt new applicants who, when established, are given the greater share of clerical assistants to relieve them of much that those of longer experience have to cope with, scarcely keeping pace with the welter of detail. Are there valuable contributions accompanying ability, not measured by the yardstick of business progress which form an important part of a well rounded library program? I speak especially of the library in a smaller college which I believe should be the intellectual and spiritual heart of the institution.

Perhaps the reason for discounting length of service is that some older librarians, particularly if they have not had a varied experience, grow stale amid the welter of detail. A rather obvious remedy, mentioned occasionally by the subjects, is that education, formal and informal, should continue throughout the librarian's career. This would go far toward keeping older librarians from becoming stultified with detail and from railing at the new library school graduates because they have little taste for this preoccupation with the means rather than the ends of library work. It would seem that academic administrations would find it an economy in the long run to provide time for such activities as attendance at institutes and short courses, staff reading programs, and sabbatical leaves if these would prevent what appears to be an occupational disease (particularly among technical process librarians). Whether or not in-service training would be an acceptable remedy, failure to make efficient use of the last half of the librarian's career and to reward continued intellectual and professional growth after age fifty is a serious problem here, as it is in most other occupational groups.

The reference to the small college in the quotation above suggests another basic finding of the survey, that the personnel conditions in smaller institutions need further study. Head librarians of such institutions tend to be isolated from the rest of the academic community, to have an uncertain perception of their role, and, in some instances, to be unhappy. Academic librarianship has been successful to a considerable extent in developing into a self-regulating, closed profession. In the opinion of most subjects of the survey, an opinion shared by the writer, this is desirable and should be continued further. However, there are limits to the benefits to be derived by emphasizing the unique role of the librarian, and these limits are most strongly seen in the case of the smaller systems.

As the sociologist Everett Hughes points out, "specialization and the closed profession should be instruments, not ends in themselves." There should be enough "circulation" to "keep new recruits coming into it... which will make for a large enough group of collaborators to stimulate one another to get the work... done."[18] The few respondents who were willing to talk explicitly about status problems usually take a leaf from Hughes' book. Faculty rank, for example, is desired, not to make professional sociologists or historians out of librarians, but, rather, to provide liaison between teaching faculty and the library staff:

> ...organized so as to function regularly and continually, by planned regular informative meetings between representatives of departments and the professional library staff. This would make for more efficient operation of the library from all points: reference, circulation, acquisitions, cataloging.

Significantly, the writer of the above is a head order librarian of a state college and is a woman.

Promotion of better communication with members of other professions and academic disciplines on the campus is another reason for urging continued education throughout the career of the academic librarian. A female librarian of mature years who heads the library of a liberal arts college of moderate size recommends:

> ...more emphasis on service. Present emphasis on hours and rights and privileges is important, but there should, also, be

equal emphasis upon service and responsibility. More emphasis upon graduate study in diversified liberal arts fields after the library degree is captured. Such work... need not result in a Ph.D., but would better enable college librarians to advance with the faculty. There is a tendency for librarians to believe that the library degree is the highest accomplishment necessary. I am thinking of such study to be continued throughout one's library career.

A social science librarian discussed the matter of intellectual isolation of the librarian as it relates to the relatively recent tendency to organize libraries on a subject-area basis. This woman entered librarianship rather late in life (at forty-one years of age) on the death of her husband. She hoped work in a university library would permit her "to keep in touch with the world of scholarship" and to "develop abilities in a selected field." She has been rather disappointed in this and feels that a "closer relationship of the library to the academic function of the college or university" is needed. Her remarks, though extensive and bitter, are worth reproducing.

> Staffing and organization of libraries in a way comparable to teaching departments to allow for advancement of subject specialists would justify more advanced scholarly training for the librarian. Seldom is there an opportunity on the job to develop the skill in bibliographic techniques and research methods, knowledge of the book trade and of book resources nationally that the library ought to be able to offer through its staff, to the academic community. What is the beginning librarian usually doing? Writing out fine slips, or prodding pages to shelve books. How many libraries allow for a leave on pay during which the librarian might get some experience in research or bibliographic work? The leave is not supported because the librarian has not reached a level of scholarly achievement that will justify it. And the librarian is told, as I was, "the Library does not encourage further study because we do not have a classification plan that provides for positions beyond the Master's level. It is assumed you are trained when you come to us."
>
> This makes for a very dead-ended professional situation, except for the limited number who go into the advanced administrative posts. In an institution with an instructional staff of 95 men in the social sciences, it is felt that one librarian at the master's level is all that can be afforded to staff the reference and service division of the library's social science work.

Implications of Findings   115

Except among librarians themselves I do not see much tendency toward changes that would remedy this condition. Consequently it seems reasonable to work toward abandoning scholarly and subject training for librarians, emphasizing technical and administrative training only.

This reaction is an extreme one and the last paragraph is undoubtedly said in irony. However, it seems evident that academic librarianship could make a more sophisticated and creative contribution to academic life than it is now making. Greater opportunity for the continuous education of librarians throughout their careers would certainly be one means for improving this situation.

It is not surprising that the sharper complaints about the isolated position of the librarian and about a "dead-ended professional situation" should come from women. Because the academic community is predominantly masculine, it is easier for a man to, in Selznick's words, "transcend his specialism"[19] in librarianship and communicate with other specialists than it is for a woman. As a result, the profession is becoming masculinized despite the fact that female librarians have personality qualifications for the work as good as, or better than, those of men. Except for such simple statements as "women in professional library work should be given equal recognition and equal respect," respondents do not suggest remedies for this situation other than to exhort library schools not to foist male administrators upon them until the bright young men are professionally dry behind the ears. The reasons for this are many and this tendency is not restricted to librarianship.

The social mechanisms by which men are granted advantages over women have been well described by Caplow[20] and need not be repeated in detail here. Allusion has already been made to the possibility that the establishment of a middle level of service might bring more women into the profession. Liberal policies on the part of library administrations in regard to in-service training and education and to participation in professional activities might keep such recruits in the profession and open more opportunities for the use of their abilities.

Speaking from a sociological point of view, Parsons contends that the tendency for librarians "to be correct, meticulous, inoffensive, and 'helpful' in a non-assertive way" is associated with the predominantly feminine composition of the profession. He says, generally speaking:

> ...there is a tendency for women to gravitate into "supportive" types of occupational role, where functions of "helpfulness" to the incumbent of more assertive and ultimately, in the social function sense, more responsible roles is a major keynote.[21]

Parsons would probably view the finding that the academic branch of librarianship is being masculinized to a greater degree than formerly as an indication that it is becoming more aggressive and less conservative. Although it is probably true in terms of the social role that women are expected to be less aggressive than men, the psychological data of Chapter V indicated that, in their perception of themselves, female librarians were typically at least as dynamic in their outlook as their male colleagues.

Among the things that women themselves might do more frequently if they wish to improve their lot in the profession is to participate in scholarly and professional activities, i.e., work in professional organizations, engage in research, and publish the results. The record of the men in these activities is better than that of the women for the same reason that they tend more frequently to seek higher degrees. This is the higher economic and status motivation of the man, for whom librarianship is virtually always a primary and permanent career activity, whereas for women it may be a temporary one, pending marriage, or a supplemental one to the career of a husband.

Although most academic librarians participate in professional organizations to at least the degree of belonging to one or more associations and attending an occasional meeting, they seem not to place much confidence in the ability of such organizations to improve the profession, or if they do, they do not say much about it. Perhaps the oligarchical nature of leadership in such associations—a tendency by no means limited to library organizations—is responsible. Probably the principle of "little breeds less" operates here. The personality inventory indicated that academic librarians generally lack initiative. Thus it would seem that it is incumbent upon head librarians to encourage members of their staffs to accept committee assignments rather than to take the easy way out and do all the work themselves. The more obvious need is for more money for staff travel, yet only one librarian commented on this:

> There are few professional meetings of importance where one does not see the heads of large libraries or deans of larger library schools. One rarely encounters the heads of smaller libraries or teachers in the lower ranks of library school teaching. Yet these people provide service to those who need it most and teach classes with the largest number of students. Such practices can not advance the best possible service for a democratic society. We all know this but who does anything about it?... These comments are made objectively because I am and have been fortunate enough to work for institutions which provide travel expenses to conferences and paid me a

up and no commonsense approach to their work; no understanding that they must fit into an organization that has been operating long before they came along and will continue to operate long after they depart. Enthusiasm without judgment doesn't add up to much.

Another major dilemma of librarianship is implicit in the above quotation, which, as usual, places all the responsibility on the professional school. Actually, more responsibility should be assumed by practitioners. It has been shown here that early recruitment and "socialization" into the profession through contact with enlightened practicing librarians has produced today's most aggressive and successful librarians. Furthermore, no matter how well financed or staffed, library schools simply cannot take over the task of preparing a specific librarian for work in a specific library system. For the beginner, there is simply no substitute for on-the-job training. Field work, as part of library school training, is a step in the right direction, but it is, of necessity, much too limited. Since the first professional year is, in fact, an internship for most librarians, the training and indoctrination aspects of it should be emphasized. However, without even considering the financial problems, the barriers to the establishment of such programs, even in the largest libraries, are formidable. Not least among these barriers is, as we have seen, the shortage of supervisors with the talent and inclination for initiating the neophyte into the role of librarian.

Furthermore, the older librarian's concept of the mission of his profession is frequently too narrow or clouded to be inspiring to the young. The purpose of internship training, of activity by professional organizations in setting standards, and of administrations in adopting liberal policies for permitting refresher training of older librarians should be as much spiritual as technical. Referring to European models, one science branch librarian put it this way:

Having spent my life in college and university communities, I am impressed by the improvement in modern library education. But through the years, my greatest criticism is of tight horizons, closed minds and regimentation in thinking even on the professional level. At the same time unforgettable are superb intellects I have encountered at Yale, Cornell, New York Public Library, Ohio State, Illinois, and in Europe.... Pondering this later, I believe the systems are good, perhaps not perfect. The impact upon the observer must come in great part from inspiration and spirit instead of mere regimentation or organization.

122 The Career of the Academic Librarian

The letter of transmittal for the questionnaire that started this survey asked three questions:

> What are the characteristics of successful academic librarians? From what backgrounds have they come? How did they happen to choose this occupation?

In many tables and much text, answers to these questions have been presented. However, one respondent succeeded in summarizing the study and answering the underlying question in one paragraph. He said:

> The successful academic librarian has to be a person who is willing to adapt to change, to hold some strong beliefs concerning his profession and is willing to absorb all the knowledge presented by others, then decide for himself in which direction he wants to throw his personal efforts and then proceed... with all means at his command.

SUMMARY

Suggestions for improvement in library science education include: (1) forging stronger ties between the general and the professional-technical phases; (2) encouragement of able young people to make an early commitment to librarianship as a career, e.g., by more emphasis on undergraduate work in library science, with the possible loss in general education to be restored by a greater provision for it in the graduate professional program; (3) provision of richer in-service education for experienced librarians who do not intend to secure the doctorate; and (4) additional study of the controversial proposal that education appropriate for a "middle service" be offered.

Improvement in the profession cannot be left to the library schools alone. The example set by older practitioners is crucial in establishing the image by which bright young people judge the career possibilities of librarianship. Since many librarians, who are otherwise competent, lack aptitude for supervising and training others, on-the-job training of student assistants and subprofessionals must be carefully planned to make optimum use of those librarians who do have this gift. Rewarding specialized competence, as opposed to general administrative ability, is essential if a maximum contribution is to be secured from both men and women. Leadership in an emerging profession, such as academic librarianship, calls for statesmanship which, as Selznick puts it, goes "beyond efficiency."[30]

NOTES

[1] "For a good many years the library schools have been the whipping boys of the profession."—Lawrence Clark Powell, "Education for Academic Librarianship," in Bernard Berelson, ed., *Education for Librarianship;* papers presented at the Library Conference, University of Chicago, Aug. 16-21, 1948 (Chicago: American Library Assn., 1949), p.133.

[2] This confirms the findings of Agnes L. Reagan, *A Study of Factors Influencing College Students To Become Librarians* ("ACRL Monograph," No.21 [Chicago: Assn. of College and Research Libraries, American Library Assn., 1958]), p.95.

[3] Everett C. Hughes, *Men and Their Work* (Glencoe, Ill.: Free Press, 1958), p.42-55.

[4] Talcott Parsons, "Implications of the [Fiske] Study," in J. Periam Danton, ed., *The Climate of Book Selection* (Berkeley: Univ. of California School of Librarianship, 1959), p.87.

[5] cf. Ralph Linton, quoted in Ralph C. Ross and Ernest van den Haag, *Fabric of Society* (New York: Harcourt, 1957), p.148-50.

[6] Talcott Parsons, *op. cit.*, p.77.

[7] Lester Asheim, ed., *The Core of Education for Librarianship* (Chicago: American Library Assn., 1954), p.4.

[8] *Ibid.*, p.51.

[9] This program is described in Cecil K. Byrd, "School for Administrators: The Rutgers Carnegie Project," *College and Research Libraries*, 20:130-33, 153 (March 1959).

[10] J. Periam Danton, *Education for Librarianship: Criticisms, Dilemmas, and Proposals* (New York: School of Library Service, Columbia Univ., 1946), p.23-35; Lesley M. Heathcote, "More on Middle-Level Training," *Library Journal*, 84:2106 (July 1959).

[11] Jim Ranz, comp., "College and University Library Statistics, 1958/59," *College and Research Libraries*, 21:25 (Jan. 1960).

[12] J. Periam Danton, *Education for Librarianship* (New York: School of Library Service, Columbia Univ., 1946), p.15.

[13] "University of Michigan, Department of Library Science, Courses in Library Science, 1959-1960" (*University of Michigan Official Publications*, 61, No.27:16 [Aug. 31, 1959]).

[14] Everett C. Hughes, *op. cit.*, p.131-38. However, Hughes does not entirely support the idea set forth here regarding the importance to the librarian of having had experience in research. It may well be that his criticisms have more validity for public librarianship than for academic. He declares that "a piece of research done as part of training for promotion to a position where one will no longer have to do research may probably have some of the faults of a diagnosis done with an eye on what diagnostic procedures the patient can pay for," p.137-38.

[15] Herbert Bisno gives a well-reasoned discussion of the false dichotomy between professional and general education for social workers in his *The Place of Undergraduate Curriculum in Social Work Education*, (New York: Council on Social Work Education, A Project Report of the Curriculum Study, Vol. 2 1959), p.21-37.

[16] Alice I. Bryan, *The Public Librarian: A Report of the Public Library Inquiry* (New York: Columbia Univ. Press, 1952), p.446.

[17] John F. Harvey, "Variety in the Experience of Chief Librarians," *College and Research Libraries*, 19:110 (March 1958).

[18] Everett C. Hughes, *op. cit.*, p.167.

[19] Philip Selznick, *Leadership in Administration: A Sociological Interpretation* (Evanston, Ill.: Row, Peterson, 1957), p.149. The phrase is Selznick's, but he does not relate it to sex.

[20] Theodore Caplow, *The Sociology of Work* (Minneapolis: Univ. of Minnesota Press, 1954), p.280 ff.

[21] Talcott Parsons, *op. cit.*, p.94-95.

[22] Robert K. Merton, George G. Reader, and Patricia L. Kendall, eds., *The Student Physician* (Cambridge, Mass.: For the Commonwealth Fund by Harvard Univ. Press, 1957), p.40-42; 287-93; Everett C. Hughes, *op. cit.*, p.40.

[23] Everett C. Hughes, *op. cit.*, p.23-41.

[24] T. H. Marshall, "The Recent History of Professionalism in Relation to Social Structure and Social Policy," *The Canadian Journal of Economics and Political Science*, 5:339 (Aug. 1939).

[25] *Ibid.*, p.340.

[26] Howard R. Gowen, "Business Management: A Profession?" *Annals of the American Academy of Political and Social Sciences*, 290:113 (Jan. 1955).

[27] Everett C. Hughes, *op. cit.*, p.119.

[28] *Ibid.*, p.40.

[29] A considerable proportion of both professions do fall into this category; cf. C. Wright Mills, *White Collar* (New York: Oxford Univ. Press, 1951), p.118.

[30] Philip Selznick, *op. cit.*, p.143, *et passim*.

CHAPTER VII

Developments since 1960

There is a certain advantage in having this study published some ten years after the original data were gathered. It gives the investigator an opportunity to review his work in the perspective gained through the passage of time.

Information reported in the preceding chapters was collected in 1958. The latest literature cited is dated 1960. Remarkably little has been published since then on the specific matters covered by the study. Meanwhile, academic librarianship has experienced a phenomenal growth. For example, it is estimated that new academic libraries are being established at the rate of fifty a year.[1] The corps of professional librarians has increased from 9000 in 1959-60 to an estimated 12,500 in 1965-66, a 39 percent gain.[2] The increase in complexity of the tasks performed by academic librarians and in the challenges facing them is difficult to state quantitatively. However, mere mention of the word "automation" is enough to suggest the extent of change facing the profession.

The dearth of data concerning the current scene is soon to be remedied by the publication of Anita R. Schiller's substantial study of the characteristics of professional personnel in academic libraries scheduled for 1968. Very little information is available concerning this study, other than that it will use 1966 data from 2300 academic librarians presently employed in the United States. Sponsored by the University of Illinois Library Research Center and financed by U.S. Office of Education grants totaling more than $30,000, it should provide a very extensive analysis of the subject.[3] By comparing 1966 data with the 1958 information reported in the present study, Schiller will be able to make important estimates of trends. Because of the way in which the 1958 samples were selected, comparative data will cover a period longer than eight years.

The median age of the librarians in this study was fifty years in 1958. Thus, they represent the older generation.

Perhaps the most significant study published since 1960 of the psychological characteristics of librarians is Stuart Baillie's study of the relationship between library school and job success completed in 1961.[4] Subjects were sixty-five graduates of a single library school, that of the University of Denver, between 1954 and 1958. Hypotheses involved the prediction of "success" in librarianship as measured by ratings made by supervisors, associates, and the librarians themselves. Baillie studied the predictive value of undergraduate and graduate grade point averages, scores on the Graduate Record Examination, and, in greatest detail, responses to the California Psychological Inventory. He also tested the hypothesis that librarians possess "normal" personalities and found that they do.[5]

Besides being restricted to graduates of a single library school, Baillie's subjects were also much younger, on the average, than those reported here. A minority (twenty-three) of Baillie's subjects were employed in academic libraries, and data for them are not analyzed separately.[6] Nor does he treat the few library executives in his study separately.

Despite these and other differences in the samples used, both studies agree that scores on personality inventory scales will "permit group prediction," but that "using these factors as the ultimate predictors of job success" is not justified.[7] This agreement holds despite the different criteria of success used. Baillie's is based on a sophisticated rating scale; the present study employs such simple (but, perhaps, more objective) criteria as salary and position in the library hierarchy. Statements about the predictive value of the instrument used in the present study rests entirely on the known consistency of personality scores over long periods of time. Baillie's adds the authority of a true before-and-after investigation.

Both studies also agree that, "on the average," librarians are psychologically normal. Although the public librarians described by Bryan in the Public Library Inquiry of 1949 were also described as "normal," one gathers the impression that they showed more deviations from typical scores on the personality inventory used than do either Baillie's subjects or those of this study.[8]

Point-by-point comparisons among studies using different inventories are suspect at best. However, one is intrigued that Baillie's "successful" librarians tended to have low scores on the "Tolerant" factor in the California Psychological Inventory scales and, thus, are described as "Narrow, Aloof, Wary, Suspicious, Retiring, Passive, Distrustful." They scored high on "Dominant" and, thus, answer to "Aggressive, Confident, Persistent, Planful, Persuasive, Verbally fluent, Self-reliant, Independent, Initiative [sic]."[9] This latter point seems to be consistent with the academic librarians' high scores on the Ghiselli self-assurance scale. The intolerance finding can be neither confirmed nor denied on the basis of the present study. It does, however, lead to the hypothesis that intolerance may be a component in the academic librarians' poor showing on the supervisory-qualities scale. One hopes that this hypothesis will not prove valid.

Baillie's research methods have been severely criticized by Robert E. Stake of the University of Illinois Office of Educational Testing.[10] Even though most of Stake's points are well taken, the present study confirms several of Baillie's general findings. This confirmation would indicate that, despite methodological flaws and the inherent difficulty of interpreting scores on subtle personality traits, Baillie did squeeze some interesting results out of a sample of only sixty-five librarians from one library school.

Although written before the appearance of Stake's criticism of Baillie, the methodological notes accompanying the present study deal with many of the same points.[11] For example, unlike Baillie's, the present work does not rely upon traditional "significance level" reasoning in discussing the meaning of the statistical data. The study reports significance-level information but uses it only as a crude "foot rule" in interpreting the differences found. Nor does this study rely much on "linear regression analysis," a method strongly criticized by Stake.[12] Statistical studies of personality do yield fruitful insights into the central tendencies of a group, but the investigator must be wary of the trap labeled "spurious precision."

For this reason, the present author continues to believe that personality-inventory methods are too imprecise to be used in formal personnel selection procedures. (Baillie seems to feel that they should be so used in combination with other measures.[13]) Even if they were more precise and reliable in individual cases, the obligation to avoid invasion of an applicant's rights to privacy severely limits the ethical use of these so-called tests.

As in any scientific endeavor, progress in the study of the librarian's personality is made by continual refinement of methods. Not only is more survey work needed, but also more work in depth (for which "clinical" is really the wrong adjective) with individual librarians. The present writer is, perhaps, unorthodox in feeling that the hypotheses developed out of survey research can be tested pragmatically. For example, does the hypothesis that many librarians lack supervisory qualities help explain some of the problems one encounters in actual staff situations?

Notice should be taken of a number of limited-purpose studies

128   The Career of the Academic Librarian

that have appeared since 1960. Robert M. Ballard has done a master's study of the "Job History of the Atlanta University School of Library Service Graduates, 1948-1959," emphasizing "factors that influence job turnover." In his report, Ballard confirms the not-too-startling finding of the present study that many of the job changes librarians make are related to the fact that most of them are women. He also confirms the finding that librarians tend not to complain about salaries, even though they do sometimes give "better salaries" as a motive for changing jobs. Paralleling those of the present study, Atlanta graduates do complain bitterly of "job stagnation and lack of opportunity for advancement." Ballard also notices the continued "brain drain" in the form of migration from the South to other areas of the country (as does the present study).[14]

Following in the footsteps of the Douglass study (discussed in Chapter V above), Nancy J. Rainwater studied ninety-four library school students' responses to the Edwards Personal Preference Schedule. Her findings confirm those of Bryan and Douglass and, in general, those of the present study.[15] However, the present study tends to emphasize differences between men and women more than Rainwater's does.

Connie E. Bolden gives some interesting information about the educational and employment backgrounds of law school librarians. Like academic librarians in the present study, law librarians also report work history in teaching more frequently than in any other area (29 percent). Law librarianship is even more demanding in the matter of degrees than other types of academic librarianship. The Joint Committee on Library Education recommends that law librarians have three degrees—general, law, and librarianship, but only 29 percent of Bolden's subjects meet this requirement. Unlike academic librarians generally, "many of the respondents indicate a desire to teach in a law school and were using librarianship as an initial step towards this goal."[16]

A short study by Frances M. Pollard of chief librarians in 143 white and 57 Negro colleges adds information not available in the present study, which did not classify its data on ethnic factors.[17]

An advantage of studying a particular cohort longitudinally is evident in Mary V. Parr's study of the 1962 classes at Drexel and Pratt library schools. The figures show that an alarming number of students who enroll in library schools never receive their degrees for other than academic reasons. Parr's rather obvious conclusion is "that admission procedures for selecting students who would eventually graduate needed improvement," but neither she nor anyone else has come up with any very radical changes in admission procedures.[18] In another study of Drexel graduates, Kenna Forsyth and John F. Harvey found that 11 of 221 (or 5 percent) of the 1960-63 graduates were "not working in the library field" in 1964.

Drexel draws almost all of its students from small, private, liberal arts colleges.[19] Table 8 of the present study indicates that in the country as a whole, many academic librarians received their first degrees from larger, state universities. Even so, liberal arts colleges produced more than their share, probably reflecting their virtual monopoly of librarian production in the area served by Drexel. Unfortunately, neither Parr's nor Forsyth's statistics are analyzed by type of library in which graduates were employed.

Confirmation of the finding here of little relationship between undergraduate major and type of position subsequently held in libraries is found in Ruth H. Rockwood's Indiana University dissertation. Rockwood studied 251 graduates of Florida State University Library School, which has a curriculum encouraging students to specialize their course work according to the kind of position they wish to obtain on graduation. In such a school "a close relationship was...discovered between choice of electives in area of specialization and subsequent positions held." This is in contrast to the lack of relationship to undergraduate major subjects. Apparently, a library school curriculum such as Florida State's encourages students to enter the academic library field.[20]

Further confirmation of Ghiselli's finding that intelligence and other attributes can be measured through apparently nonintellectual psychological inventories comes from a recent article in the *Journal of Counseling Psychology*, which, fortunately, includes librarians among the groups studied. In this study, David P. Campbell and Charles B. Johansson developed an Academic Achievement Scale by analyzing data gathered over the years by means of the Strong Vocational Interest Blank. This AACH Scale is shown to predict eventual scholastic achievement. Mean AACH score for 425 librarians tested in 1959 was sixth highest of 53 occupational groups (males only), being exceeded only by biologists, mathematicians, psychiatrists, physicists, and psychologists. The mean for librarians was higher than that, for example, for physicians and much higher than that for social science teachers.[21] This confirms the findings from the Ghiselli intelligence-scale scores in the present study. People of high intellectual ability are attracted to academic librarianship.

Campbell and Johansson also found that the "AACH Scale is more indicative of occupation selected than of performance there."[22] This parallels the finding that academic librarians are virtually all very intelligent and that the differences within the group on this trait are not related to "success" in the profession. Although Baillie and others have found that undergraduate grade point

130   The Career of the Academic Librarian

average is a good predictor of graduate school GPA, the same measure in library school does not correlate well with "success" in the profession.

> Graduate schools enroll students with superior intellectual abilities, and it is much harder to differentiate the successful and the unsuccessful candidate on the basis of intelligence alone. Other factors such as personality, experience, motivation, and interest become equally important.[23]

The work reported in Chapter V of the present study comes to the same conclusion.

U.S. Office of Education "postcensal" data on the occupational characteristics of public and school librarians in 1962 have recently been published.[24] Because the design of the present study of academic librarians differs so markedly from the demographic approach of census analysis, comparisons between the two studies are hazardous. Presumably the data in the forthcoming Schiller study of academic librarians will be more fully compatible with those for the high school and public librarians in the Office of Education studies.

With the above caveat in mind, it is possible to make a few comparative observations about academic, public, and school librarians, particularly regarding socio-economic backgrounds. Table 38 compares the family socio-economic backgrounds of the three groups of librarians as indicated by father's occupation. The interesting conclusion implied in these data is that school librarians tend to more nearly resemble schoolteachers than other types of librarians in this characteristic. This leads to the hypothesis that people attracted to school librarianship would fall between teachers and other librarians in other traits as well. For example, although the data are not directly comparable, there is a suggestion that academic librarians are more mobile than school librarians. Public librarians *were* more mobile than school librarians in 1962: "median years with present employer was 8.9 years" in the case of public librarians; for school librarians it was 11.1.[25]

There was an alarming migration out of public librarianship over a period of only two years. Between 1960 and 1962, "2,310 persons were estimated to have departed."[26] It seems reasonable to postulate that the staffs of college and university libraries have increased at the expense of those of public libraries. More work needs to be done on the attrition rates of librarianship and on movement between various segments of it.

A brief study by John Caldwell of the 1960 population of the chiefs of academic libraries with 50,000 volumes or more has

TABLE 38.
FATHER'S OCCUPATION FOR ACADEMIC, PUBLIC, AND
SCHOOL LIBRARIANS AND FOR TEACHERS' COLLEGE STUDENTS

Father's Occupation	Academic Librarians 1958*	Public Librarians 1962†	School Librarians 1962†	Teachers' College Students‡ 1929	Teachers 1960-61§
Professional and kindred	29%	25%	16%	8%	15%
White collar	41	40	33	54	29
Blue collar	30	34	50	64	56

*See Table 2.

†Henry T. Drennan and Richard L. Darling, *Library Manpower: Occupational Characteristics of Public and School Librarians* (U.S. Office of Education Publication OE-15061 [Washington, D.C.: Govt. Print. Off., 1966]), p.8, 16. Data for public and school librarians have been adjusted to correct for different treatment of the category "father no longer living" from that used in the academic library study.

‡M'ledge Moffett, *The Social Background and Activities of Teachers' College Students* ("Teachers College Contribution to Education," No.375 [New York: Teachers College, Columbia Univ., 1929]), p.26. For undisclosed reasons proportions add up to 126%; probably two or more occupations were counted for some subjects whereas in other studies only "principal" occupation is included. If one were to make a mathematical correction for this, it would have the effect of reducing further, if anything, the proportion of "Professional" fathers of teachers. Although the data for Teachers' College students were gathered in 1929, the median year of father's occupation data is about the same as that for the academic librarians.

§National Education Association, Research Division, *The American Public School Teacher, 1960-61* (Washington, D.C.: National Education Assn., 1963), p.15.

provided an opportunity to check on the effect of non-response to the questionnaire on which the 1958 study was based.[27] Caldwell studied educational attainment only and drew his data from published sources. His population was not much different from the one used here, but he was able to find educational data on 471 (or 472—there is an unexplained discrepancy in his figures), whereas the present study obtained responses from only 231. As one might expect, Table 39 shows that librarians with lesser educational attainments tended to fail to respond to the questionnaire and, hence, are under-represented in the 1958 group. The salary-level criteria used in the 1958 study probably also cut off some librarians with relatively less education.

One recent development in education for librarianship is very clearly foreshadowed in the study. A sizable number of the 1958

TABLE 39.
ACADEMIC ATTAINMENTS OF CHIEF LIBRARIANS
IN TWO SEPARATE STUDIES

Highest Degree Held	1958 Major Executives* (231)	Chief Librarians of Libraries with 50,000 or More Volumes† (472)
No degree of any kind	1%	1%
Bachelor's only (L.S. or other)	14	22
Master's in librarianship (as first or second post-baccalaureate degree)	30	27
Subject master's (with or without also having library degrees)	31	32
Doctorate (L.S. or subject)	24	19

*See Table 11 in Chapter III above.
†John Caldwell, "Degrees Held by Head Librarians of Colleges and Universities," *College and Research Libraries*, 23:227-28 (May 1962).

librarians called for more emphasis on continuing education for librarians and, especially, for a degree level between the master's and doctoral level. Furthermore, the statistical analysis showed the great importance of the old-style, sixth-year master's degree, particularly to women who wished to advance in the profession. At that time, this degree was being phased out. Now, a similar level of education is widely advocated and is being established in a number of institutions, not only in librarianship but also in other fields.[28]

Many of the 1958 librarians also called for a level of training below that of the master's. However, none of them recommended a terminal technician's program in community colleges such as are now being widely established.[29] What the librarians did want was an undergraduate library science curriculum leading to a bachelor's degree analogous to those offered by the old Type III library schools. This would not necessarily be a terminal degree, but it would supply people who would work in what might be termed a "paraprofessional" level for a few years before going on to a graduate library school. This would free the "middle service" librarians of some of the tasks requiring training, but not at the graduate level.

At present, librarians tend to be critical of specialized training programs at the community college level, fearing that they will produce people with skills that soon become obsolete and without the insights provided by sound general education. There is also the fear that people trained as technicians will be used as cheap substitutes for adequately trained librarians.[30]

No doubt the weakness in supervisory qualities of many of the librarians reported here will be cited in support of the technician training programs. Whether teaching technical skills in community college classes will produce clerks requiring less supervision than those trained in, say, business office skills has yet to be shown. Each academic library has clerical routines peculiar to itself. Thus, whatever skills are acquired in a technician program must be adapted to the local situation. Supervisory competence will continue to be required to accomplish this.

Almost entirely lacking from the responses of the 1958 group were references to the possibility of a new profession arising to challenge librarianship. Whether the cluster of skills now sometimes grouped under the title "Information Scientist" will supplant, co-exist with, supplement, or merge into librarianship as we know it is not, at the moment, foreseeable. One finding of this study, but far from unique to it, is relevant: Librarians tend to be humanistic in training and outlook; information science requires a more technological bent. What C. P. Snow described as the "two cultures" must be represented on the staffs of the automated library of the future. It would seem to be efficient to have the two points of view represented in a single profession, and library schools are introducing programs designed to bring this about.[31] No doubt the situation in 1958 continues at present: There are insufficient librarians with scientific and technical interests and training to man existing branch libraries in those subjects, to say nothing of providing automation staffs for general libraries. Recruiting people with this background is urgently required. So are programs for "converting" those whose prior interests and training have been exclusively in the humanities.

The 1958 librarians displayed only a modicum of interest in unions as a type of library organization. Unions were once thought of as inappropriate to academic life, generally, and to so genteel a profession as librarianship, particularly. Now there is a militant minority of professors and librarians who no longer hold this view.[32] Unions are concerned not only with the economic welfare of academic librarians, but also with their status on campus and with their participation in administrative decision-making. Taking their cue from the rapidly growing union movement among public school teachers, library union advocates are trying to capitalize on some of the discontent with traditional library associations as expressed by respondents to this study in 1958.

A very significant article by William J. Goode, a sociologist, on the progress, or lack thereof, of librarianship from occupation to profession first appeared in 1961 and has been reprinted at least twice since.[33] Goode's conclusion is that, sociologically speaking, "the central structural position of the librarian will not permit full professionalization." In arriving at this, some of his arguments are nominalistic. To reduce them to absurdity, he seems to be saying that because librarianship is not medicine, law, divinity, or college professorship, it cannot be fully professional. He avoids the central tenet of this study, i.e., that the status of an occupation takes on significance and prestige in proportion to the ability and willingness of its practitioners to accept, and act upon, the highest challenges inherent in it. There is no lack of such challenges in academic librarianship, as Goode takes pains to show. He attributes to "social structure" what this study finds to be a failure on the part of librarians to accept, psychologically, their proper role as professional people. The recent emergence of what may prove to be a rival profession, information science, indicates that there are high-level jobs to be done in librarianship; the lack is of people disposed to accept the responsibilities involved.

Having said this, one must hasten to add that there are, indeed, structural impediments to the full use of the considerable reservoir of talent now in librarianship. For example, Goode echoes the sentiments of many of the subjects of this study in criticizing the tendency of academic librarianship to base salary and prestige almost entirely on the assumption of administrative tasks.

Goode also hits a raw nerve when he says what was also expressed by a few of the librarians in this study:

> Perhaps one clear index of the failure to develop a clearly defined field of knowledge may be seen in the continuing and successful efforts by college and university librarians to obtain faculty status for themselves. By defining much of their task as teaching, these librarians can make a fair case for their claim to faculty status. On the other hand, if their definition of core professional problems was unique and special to the tasks of a library, they could gain all of the material advantages, which figure so prominently in their arguments, of faculty status without demanding the title of another profession.[34]

Probably most librarians would consider this a species of the "separate-but-equal" argument.[35] They would contend that librarians do not lose professional identity by assuming academic rank and title any more than, say, sociologists or historians do.

Despite notable victories and many rational arguments favoring it, it is still not clear that librarians will succeed generally in a recognized field, have had some training therein, and who have the capacity for achieving success as *persons* are best. It seems to me, therefore—if you accept these premises—that a library school program which emphasizes careful selection of students and minimizes the "professional" courses would be better than the conventional programs.

Catalogers and technical process people, on the other hand, frequently feel that indoctrination of neophytes is a primary consideration and that the image thus instilled should be of the librarian as a keeper of the art. They emphasize that part of the definition of "professional" which refers to "an intellectually based technique."[26] One catalog librarian put it this way:

> I think something should be done to interest young people in cataloging and classification at the university level. Better indoctrination should show them that working with books in various languages (for which there are no L.C. cards) provides daily variety and stimulus to use one's head. We do need more converts. After thirty-five years of cataloging, every day presents some books in which the publisher and/or the author hand me a new problem, and I think the game is worth the effort.

Public service librarians, on the other hand, stress the service ideal; subject specialists (usually branch librarians) may speak of "respect for a knowledge of the academic and scholarly materials with which they work"; administrators refer to "efficiency"; and the heads of the larger libraries sometimes do not identify themselves with library work at all but, rather, with the administrative elite of the campus (deans and department heads). The variety of possible models on which a librarian might shape his career is so great that attempts at examining statistically the data of this survey by type of position were not very successful.

This situation is not peculiar to librarianship. That touchstone profession, medicine, exhibits differing role models as between, for example, the general practitioner and the specialist, or the surgeon and the pathologist. Nevertheless, it is a closed profession with a "personality" of its own that transcends differences among its component specialties. Of it, Hughes says:

> A role is always a part of some system of interaction of human beings; it is always played opposite other roles. To play one is not to play another. One might say that the learning of the medical role consists of a separation, almost an alienation, of the student from the lay medical world; a passing through the mirror

so that one looks out on the world from behind it, and sees things as in a mirror writing. In all of the more esoteric occupations we have studied we find the sense of seeing the world in reverse.[27]

Although Hughes is probably right in criticizing library education for attempting to harden this image prematurely and in hoping that the neo-professions, with which he classifies librarianship, will continue to be somewhat fluid, the professionalization of this occupation has proceeded apace and will certainly continue to do so. The art is too complex, too intimately concerned with the need of people, to be practiced without a common mission generally recognized by its practitioners. It requires machinery for enforcing standards of practice, mechanisms for transmitting the techniques, and, finally, a sense of identity for the librarian as a person, "what we may call a culture, an etiquette, and a group within which one may attain the satisfaction of his wishes."[28]

Although he may justifiably seek rank in the academic system commensurate with his abilities and training, it is doubtful that every librarian can identify his role with that of the teaching faculty. As one respondent put it (again a technical processes librarian):

> The mistake is trying to equate library work with academic disciplines such as literature or history. Librarianship is a profession, to be sure, but in the way that law or medicine are professional.

(It should be added that this applies only to those portions of the legal and medical professions that are salaried appendages to larger bureaucratic structures rather than to independent practitioners.[29])

The first task in creating a "personality" for librarianship is to solve the problem of the place of technique. Paradoxically, it would seem that what the technical process librarians, who are most critical of the lack of technical training on the part of neophytes, are really seeing is the results of too much, rather than too little, emphasis on technical minutiae with a resultant lowering of respect for it. As a remedy, one head librarian recommends:

> More emphasis on philosophy of librarianship and less on techniques (except of cataloging, and even here there could be more emphasis on theory and a de-emphasizing of practice). What I note too frequently in library school graduates on their first job is a lack of values, of judgment, and a desire to rush into practice all the fine theories [*read* techniques (?)] they have picked

Implications of Findings 117

pretty decent salary, but travelling around, teaching in library schools and having personal contacts in many parts of the country I notice conditions which are appalling, compared with those prevailing in other professions.

Although the subjects are usually anxious that the profession develop high standards and a sense of solidarity, only one furnished a statement that recognizes the role of organizations, but it is a good statement:

> I think it extremely important that professional attributes be developed in or begin in the library school. I am not sure that it is the intent of every library school to emphasize the service aspect of librarianship, and to train to professional competence. I noted however that not enough emphasis was placed on the professional responsibility toward professional organizations, responsibility to read widely and deeply in literature. In every respect I believe that the Michigan School of Library Science was adequate on these points, but I think it should be emphasized even more that a librarian must continually challenge his mind through professional reading and must continually apply a critical mind to his professional activity. It can only be done if habits that I call professional are firmly instilled. It is much more than a job, being a librarian, it is a vocation directed very much to the heart of the whole educational process. Nothing less than a passion for the work involved is needed. Anything else or less results in mediocrity and self-complacency.

This is an unusual statement by an unusual librarian. The author is a member of a Catholic religious order who has been working in libraries since the age of fifteen and who, in 1958, at the age of thirty-five headed a liberal arts college library after receiving a master of arts in library science and doing some work toward a doctorate. Here is a man with a triple vocation: to the church, to education, and to librarianship. In his case, commitment to librarianship has certainly not precluded other commitments but, rather, is part and parcel of them. In describing the reasons he chose librarianship as a profession, he gives a succinct description of the process Merton calls "socialization," to which Hughes refers as the development of an occupational "personality type,"[22] which this librarian's church calls "vocation," and which he dubs simply a "mission" (again reflecting the religious model):

> At first I was fascinated by the complexity and detail of library work. I worked under professional librarians from the beginning

who saw my keen interest and who trained me not only in technique but in reasons. I see it now as a sort of educational mission.

Many persons who are considered "professional" librarians never get beyond the first stage of this process, but those who do are the ones who attract desirable recruits from among student assistants.

THE LIBRARIAN'S PERSONALITY

Social psychologists use the word "personality" to describe the outlook on life peculiar to a particular occupation, the sense of mission so well exemplified by the priest-librarian in the preceding paragraph. Other psychologists use the word in a different way in referring to traits that more frequently characterize one group of people than another. The emphasis of the first definition is upon acquisition of attitudes as a result of joining an occupation; the second, on the selection of people who already have certain characteristics either in fully developed or rudimentary form.[23] The inventory used in this survey reflects both aspects of "personality." However, it would appear that librarianship tends to select rather than to develop personality. In the words of T. H. Marshall's classic article on professionalism, "this middle-class group of the lesser professions and the salaried employments has many common features,"[24] and these features are reflected in personality measurements. However, it seems desirable that academic librarianship develop a "personality" in the sense favored by the social psychologist, for, again quoting Marshall, practitioners of this type of profession "are relatively free from the spirit of pecuniary and business employments, and in addition it is their business to study human needs and to construct a scale of human values."[25]

Although no easier to solve, the problem of selection of people on the basis of personality is easier to formulate than that of developing a professional "role" or "self-image." One head librarian of a large university recommends that selection of students should take precedence over professional acculturation in library schools:

> For the more important positions in university libraries qualities of perception, comprehension, inventiveness, communicativeness and in some cases, a substantial knowledge of the literature, problems, and methods of a field of scholarship are of first importance. Development of these is better done in programs other than those of existing library schools. For those positions, persons who are capable of graduate work in

obtaining full identification with the rest of the faculty of colleges and universities, both *de facto* and *de jure*. However, the situation may be changing. The active discontent with the *status quo* on many campuses, exemplified by the decision of a highly vocal minority to join unions, may be replacing the genteel apathy about status that was evident in this and other studies of the profession ten or more years ago. What is lacking is information, in depth, of the real commitments of academic librarians. To what standards do they really subscribe? With what groups on campus and in society do they identify? Should they be encouraged to change these affiliations in the interest of a higher professional and economic status?

There are as yet no clear signs that the rather strong words *"anomie"* and "normlessness," applied to some members of the 1958 group, also fit the younger generation of academic librarians. Are they (1) moving toward a separate psychological identity, (2) moving toward full acceptance of the ideals and standards of the majority group, the professoriate, or (3) content to remain unaffiliated with any group? (Incidentally the third position is not without its attractions in terms of individual intellectual autonomy.)

The respondents to this study were fully aware of most of the aspects of the problem of library manpower that the American Library Association finally tried to face in its 1967 conference. In fact, the 1958 group was more concerned with the qualitative aspects of manpower than many of the authors of the preliminary papers for the conference.[36] However, during the "study-discussion" session of the program, "there were pleas for definitions of professional and nonprofessional roles and for analysis of present library tasks."[37] Studies such as the present one and the forthcoming Schiller report may not tell us all we want to know about the characteristics of the present staffs of academic libraries, but we know much less about what talents are actually needed in today's college and university libraries, to say nothing of tomorrow's. A study underway now, not by a library organization but by the American Council of Learned Societies, may furnish some of this information.[38] Most studies so far have tried to tell us how many librarians the nation needs or will need. What is required now is an answer to the more difficult question, "What kind of librarians?"[39]

In conclusion, the sketchy data that has been published since the completion of this study suggests the following hypothesis for future testing: If general demographic tendencies in the nation as a whole are taken into account, there is relatively little difference between the characteristics of the group of librarians studied here and those of their younger colleagues. The new crop is not a "new breed." We seem to be aware that a "new breed" is needed, but just what it should be like and how it should be bred is not clear.[40]

NOTES

[1] Theodore Samore, "College and University Library Statistics and Legislation: Review and Report," *Bowker Annual of Library and Book Trade Information,* 1967 (New York: Bowker, 1967), p.21.

[2] *Ibid.,* p.24.

[3] "Illinois Library Research Center To Study Academic Library Personnel," *Library Journal,* 90:5225-26 (Dec. 1, 1965); "Awards, Grants, and Gifts," *College and University Libraries News,* 28:225 (Oct. 1967); letter from Anita R. Schiller, Nov. 29, 1967; Manpower Research Project, School of Library and Information Services, University of Maryland, *Newsletter,* 1:5 (Jan. 1968).

[4] Stuart Baillie, *Library School and Job Success* ("University of Denver Studies in Librarianship," Vol. 1, No.3 [Denver: Univ. of Denver School of Librarianship, 1964]). 176p.

[5] *Ibid.,* p.74.

[6] *Ibid.,* p.35.

[7] *Ibid.,* p.72.

[8] *Ibid.,* p.22-24, 77.

[9] *Ibid.,* p.78-79.

[10] Robert E. Stake, in "Review of Current Research," *Journal of Education for Librarianship,* 5:137-41 (Fall, 1964).

[11] See Appendix II, below.

[12] Robert E. Stake, *op. cit.,* p.138.

[13] Stuart Baillie, *op. cit.,* p.85, but compare this statement with his remarks on p.72 which seem to indicate the opposite point of view.

[14] Robert M. Ballard, "Job History of the Atlanta University School of Library Service Graduates, 1948-1959" (M.S. thesis, Univ. of Atlanta, 1961), p.34.

[15] Nancy J. Rainwater, "A Study of Personality Traits of Ninety-Four Library School Students as Shown by the Edwards Personal Preference Schedule" (M.L.S. thesis, Univ. of Texas, 1962), p.32. See also Anne McMahon, *The Personality of the Librarian: Prevalent Social Values and Attitudes toward the Profession* ("Occasional Papers in Librarianship," No.5 [Adelaide: Libraries Board of South Australia, 1967]). 127p. Review by Norman Horrocks in *Library Journal,* 93:3530-31 (Oct. 1968), states that "Miss McMahon examines the personality characteristics of the 30 professional librarians in the state of Tasmania during May-July 1965. Her findings generally agree with those of R. R. Douglass (1957) and P. D. Morrison (1960) in their doctoral theses which dealt with Americal librarians."

[16] Connie E. Bolden, "The Educational and Employment Backgrounds of Law School Librarians," (M.S. in L.S. thesis, Univ. of North Carolina, 1966), p.38-39, 40-48.

[17] Frances M. Pollard, "Characteristics of Negro College Chief Librarians," *College and Research Libraries,* 25:281-83 (July 1964).

[18] Mary V. Parr, "Whatever Happened to the Class of 1962?," *College and Research Libraries,* 28:208-16 (May 1967).

[19] Kenna Forsyth and John F. Harvey, "Drexel Library School Students:

Where Do They Come From and Where Do They Go," *College and Research Libraries*, 26:138-44 (March 1965). Another study of Drexel alumni also confirms several of the findings of the present study; see Mary Parr and Marilyn Filderman, "Some Characteristics of Successful Alumni," *College and Research Libraries*, 27:225-26, 238 (May 1966).

[20] Ruth H. Rockwood, "The Relationship between the Professional Preparation and Subsequent Types of Library Positions Held by a Selected Group of Library School Graduates" (Ed.D. dissertation, Indiana Univ., 1960), *Dissertation Abstracts*, 21:2726-27 (March 1961).

[21] David P. Campbell and Charles B. Johansson, "Academic Interests, Scholastic Achievements and Eventual Occupations," *Journal of Counseling Psychology*, 13:422 (Winter, 1966).

[22] *Ibid.*, p.416.

[23] Stuart Baillie, *op. cit.*, p.80.

[24] Henry T. Drennan and Richard L. Darling, *Library Manpower: Occupational Characteristics of Public and School Librarians* (U.S. Office of Education Publication OE-15061 [Washington, D.C.: Govt. Print. Off., 1966]).

[25] *Ibid.*, p.11, 19.

[26] *Ibid.*, p.12.

[27] John Caldwell, "Degrees Held by Head Librarians of Colleges and Universities," *College and Research Libraries*, 23:227-28, 260 (May 1962).

[28] Raynard C. Swank, "Sixth-Year Curricula and the Education of Library School Faculties," *Journal of Education for Librarianship*, 8:14-19 (Summer, 1967).

[29] American Library Association, Joint Ad Hoc Committee of Library Administration Division and Library Education Division on Sub-Professional or Technician Class of Library Employees, *Report* (Chicago: A.L.A., 1967). 11p. "...proposes some basic definitions and classification specifications, including statements of typical duties for the sub-professional or technician class of library employees" (p.1).

[30] See, e.g., Samuel Sass, "Library Technicians—Instant Librarians?" *Library Journal*, 92:2122-26 (June 1, 1967).

[31] Robert M. Hayes, "Data Processing in the Library School Curriculum," *ALA Bulletin*, 61:662-69 (June 1967).

[32] Karl Nyren, "Libraries and Labor Unions," *Library Journal*, 92:2115-21 (June 1, 1967). (p.2116-17 deal specifically with academic library unions.)

[33] William J. Goode, "The Librarian: From Occupation to Profession?," *The Library Quarterly*, 31:306-18 (Oct. 1961). Reprinted in Howard M. Vollmer and Donald L. Mills, eds., *Professionalization* (Englewood Cliffs, N.J.: Prentice-Hall, 1966), p.34-43, immediately following an article on "The Profession of Theft." Citations here are to the reprint in *ALA Bulletin*, 61:544-55 (May 1967).

[34] *Ibid. (ALA Bulletin)*, p.550.

[35] See, e.g., Robert B. Downs, "Place of College Librarians in the Academic World," *California Librarian*, 28:101-6 (April 1967).

[36] An unpaged pamphlet by Henry T. Drennan and Sarah R. Reed (no place, publisher, or date given) entitled "Library Manpower," distributed at the conference, gives an interesting statistical review. Interpretative articles appeared in *ALA Bulletin*, May 1967; *Wilson Library Bulletin*, April 1967; and *Library Journal*, June 1, 1967.

[37] "Manpower" (reports from the San Francisco conference), *ALA Bulletin*, 61:838 (July-Aug. 1967).

[38] Foster E. Mohrhardt, "Libraries Unlimited," *ALA Bulletin*, 61:814 (July-Aug. 1967).

[39] The first issue of the *Newsletter* of the Manpower Research Project of the School of Library and Information Services, University of Maryland, arrived just as this paper was going to press. It carries an annotated bibliography of library and information-science manpower studies in progress or completed during 1963-67. It contains little specific information about academic librarians not reported here, but it does list studies-in-progress of various other types of librarians that were not included in the present account.

[40] The following articles, among others, are of interest: "New Librarian," *Newsweek*, 68:85-86 (July 25, 1966); Richard M. Gummere, Jr., "Toward a New Breed of Librarians," *Wilson Library Bulletin*, 41:810-13 (April 1967).

APPENDIX I

Questionnaire and Other Instruments Used in Gathering Data

SCHOOL OF LIBRARIANSHIP
OFFICE OF THE DEAN
BERKELEY 4, CALIFORNIA

April 15, 1958

Dear Colleague:

    The attached materials come to you from Mr. Perry D. Morrison who has been advanced to candidacy for the doctor's degree here, and whose dissertation study has been approved by the Faculty of the School of Librarianship and the special committee on his dissertation. We believe that the project will add substantially to our knowledge of the nature of academic librarianship. Your cooperation in supplying Mr. Morrison with data will be greatly appreciated by him and by us.

Sincerely yours,

J. Periam Danton
Dean

JPD:bj

Appendix I

> Mailing Address:
> School of Librarianship
> University of California
> Berkeley 4, California
> April, 1958

What are the characteristics of successful academic librarians? From what backgrounds have they come? How did they happen to choose this occupation? Answers to these and related questions would not only be of general interest to the profession but would also provide data useful for recruiting and guidance purposes.

Recent studies have answered similar questions regarding scientists and other scholars,* considerable data about the public librarian are available in the reports of the Public Library Inquiry, but college and university librarians have not been systematically studied heretofore. The aim of my doctoral project is to fill this gap.

The enclosed forms will give you an opportunity to reflect upon your experience in librarianship and thus provide the basis for this portrayal of the American academic librarian. These materials are being sent to a limited, carefully-chosen sample of librarians engaged in various kinds of activity in college and university libraries. Virtually complete returns must be received before reliable conclusions may be drawn. Therefore, your participation is earnestly requested.

Two blanks are enclosed: an Information Sheet and a Self-Description Inventory. The latter presents an intriguing challenge. It is of a so-called "forced-choice" nature and requires that a decision be made on each pair of adjectives regardless of how nearly equal the alternatives may at first appear.

The blanks need not be signed. In order to insure anonymity, please return the completed papers in the stamped envelope provided. Then place the postal card into the mail separately to indicate that you have returned the materials.

The results of this study will be fully reported to the profession. Meanwhile, please accept my thanks for your cooperation.

> Sincerely yours,
>
> Perry D. Morrison

*R. H. Knapp, Origins of American Scientists (1952)
_____, The Younger American Scholar (1953)
K. E. Clark, America's Psychologists (1957).

INFORMATION SHEET

1. What is the full title of your present position? (e.g. "assistant catalog librarian")_____ In what type of institution? (e.g. "liberal arts college".)_____.

2. How many people in full-time equivalent are under your direction? (include both those you supervise directly and those who report through a chain of command). Please give approximate number.

   ___Student assistants.   ___Clerical & sub-professional.   ___Professional.

3. Please check the range in which your present annual salary in full-time equivalent falls.

   ___Less than $4,000.   ___$5,000 to 5,999.   ___$7,000 to 7,999
   ___$4,000 to $4,999.   ___$6,000 to 6,999.   ___$8,000 or more.

4. When did you first think about becoming a librarian? Finally decide?

   First considered   Decided

   ___   ___   Before high school
   ___   ___   During high school
   ___   ___   As an undergraduate in college
   ___   ___   After college

5. Do you have a clear memory of the reasons you chose librarianship as a career?   ___yes.   ___no. (If yes, please state them below).

   Who, if anyone, inspired or influenced your decision? (e.g. school teacher, public librarian, etc.) _____.

6. In what other full-time occupations (if any) did you engage before becoming a librarian?_____.
   Approximately how old were you when you obtained your first full-time position in a library? _____. Was it a professional position? ___yes. ___no.
   In how many different libraries have you held positions?_____.

7. Do you feel that perhaps you should have chosen an occupation other than librarianship?   ___Yes.   ___No. If so, what occupation?_____.

8. All things considered, what do you personally like best about library work?

   What do you like least?

9. What kind of work did your father do for a living when you were eighteen years of age (or if he was deceased or retired by then, what was his last occupation?) Please give a full title and description, e.g. "high school chemistry teacher", "lathe operator in a machine shop", "owner-operator of a small farm"._____.

Appendix I

10. In what kind of place did you live the longest when you were in grade school (age approx. 6-13)? In high school (age approx. 14-18)?

Grade School	High School	
___	___	Rural area
___	___	Small town (up to 2500)
___	___	Small city (2500 to 25,000)
___	___	Medium city (25,000 to 100,000)
___	___	Big city (100,000 to 500,000)
___	___	Metropolis (over 500,000)

    In what state of the U.S. or what foreign country was it?
    During grade school:_____. During high school:_____.

11. How much formal education did your parents have? (check the highest level achieved by each parent).

Father	Mother	
___	___	Some grade school
___	___	Grade school graduate
___	___	Some high school
___	___	High school graduate
___	___	Business or trade school
___	___	Some college
___	___	College graduate
___	___	Graduate school or professional school.

12. Please check the phrase which you think best describes your family's financial situation most of the time before you were 21 years old.

    ___ Sometimes had difficulty getting the necessities
    ___ Had all the necessities but not many luxuries
    ___ Comfortable but not well-to-do
    ___ Well-to-do
    ___ Wealthy

13. Please give information as to your education:

    Undergraduate institutions attended.   Dates.   Degrees.   Major subjects.
    _____   _____   _____   _____
    _____   _____   _____   _____
    _____   _____   _____   _____

    Graduate institutions attended.
    (exclusive of library schools)
    _____   _____   _____   _____
    _____   _____   _____   _____
    _____   _____   _____   _____

    Library schools attended (include both first-professional and advanced work)
                                              Dates.   Degrees or certificates.
    _____   _____   _____
    _____   _____   _____
    _____   _____   _____

Questionnaire and Other Instruments Used

Note: The next three questions concern your <u>opinions</u> about education in general and of librarians in particular.

14. In general, what do you think the main purposes of an undergraduate college education should be? Place an "H" before the <u>two</u> most important items in your opinion.

    ___ Provide vocational or pre-professional training; develop skills and techniques directly applicable to one's career.
    ___ Develop one's ability to get along with different kinds of people.
    ___ Develop one's critical facilities and his appreciation for ideas.
    ___ Develop special competence in a particular academic discipline.
    ___ Develop one's knowledge of, and interest in, community and world problems.
    ___ Help develop one's moral capacities, ethical standards and values.
    ___ Prepare one for a happy marriage and family life.
    ___ Other (specify)_____.

    Now please go back and check (✓) any items in which you feel that your undergraduate experience was deficient. <u>Underline</u> items in which it was particularly strong.

15. The following are a few important things a student preparing for academic librarianship might get out of library science courses. Place an "H" before the <u>four</u> items which are, in your opinion, the <u>most</u> important.

    ___ Knowledge of the ways in which libraries are organized.
    ___ Knowledge of the origin and development of academic libraries.
    ___ Appreciation of the library's place in higher education.
    ___ Practical help in the techniques of reference, circulation, acquisitions, cataloging, etc.
    ___ Knowledge applicable to the problems of one special type of institution of higher education (Agricultural, liberal arts, etc.)
    ___ General acquaintance with important titles in each of the broad curricular fields – social science, humanities, science, technology.
    ___ Attitudes of accuracy, system and speed in performance of duties.
    ___ Knowledge of the ways of evaluating the use made of library materials.
    ___ Knowledge of the history of language, books, and printing.
    ___ Other (specify)_____.

    If you had library school training please go back and check (✓) any items in which you feel it was deficient. <u>Underline</u> any which were <u>over</u>-emphasized as far as you are concerned.

16. Which three library schools, in your opinion, seem to produce the greatest number of outstanding academic librarians? _____, _____, _____.

17. In finding library positions, how much help have you personally received from each of the following?

    Much   Some   Little
    ____   ____   ____   Placement services of a library school
    ____   ____   ____   Other placement services and agencies
    ____   ____   ____   Advertisements and notices
    ____   ____   ____   Letters of inquiry to prospective employers
    ____   ____   ____   Individual contacts through friends and associates
    ____   ____   ____   Other (specify)_____.

Appendix I

18. In which of the following categories have you had writings of a professional, scholarly, or general nature published? Give number of items.

    Professional   Scholarly   General

    _____   _____   _____   Articles
    _____   _____   _____   Reviews
    _____   _____   _____   Books and monographs
    _____   _____   _____   Other (specify)_____.

    Other publication activity (editorships, etc.) _____.

19. To what professional and scholarly organizations do you belong? (e.g. state or regional library associations, A.L.A. American Historical Assn., American Assn. of University Professors, etc.) How active have you been in each? (Use other side of sheet if more space needed).

Organization	Usually attend meetings	Serve on Committees	Officer or committee chairman
_____	_____	_____	_____
_____	_____	_____	_____
_____	_____	_____	_____

    To what religious, civic, fraternal or social organizations do you belong?

_____	_____	_____	_____
_____	_____	_____	_____
_____	_____	_____	_____

20. In addition to library work, do you do other types of work part-time? (e.g. teaching history). ___yes. ___no. If yes, what kind of work? _____

21. What is your present age? _____ . Your sex? __Male __Female __Married?

22. Do you have suggestions for improving librarianship or library education? ___Yes. ___No. (If yes, please write them on the other side of this sheet.)

The next, and final, item of this study is a Self-Description Inventory adapted from one developed by Dr. Edwin E. Ghiselli of the Psychology Department of the University of California. This instrument is one of the "forced-choice" type. It has been found that even though some of the choices may be perplexing, valid results are not obtained unless a decision is made on each and every pair of adjectives. If a choice is particularly difficult to make, please mark your best guess and place a question mark beside the item (add a comment if you wish.) As indicated in the cover letter, anonymity of responses will be strictly observed.

PLEASE PROCEED TO THE INVENTORY ON THE NEXT SHEET.

For tabulation purposes – please do not write here.
Type of library 1a 1b 2 3 4 Sample number 1 2 3

Questionnaire and Other Instruments Used 145

SELF-DESCRIPTION INVENTORY

The purpose of this inventory is to obtain a picture of the traits you believe you possess and to see how you describe yourself. There are no right or wrong answers, so try to describe yourself as accurately and honestly as you can. You are to check (✓) one word in each of the following pairs.

In each of the pairs of words below check the one you think MOST describes you.

1. __capable __discreet	10. __planful __resourceful	19. __sincere __calm	28. __conscientious __quick
2. __understanding __thorough	11. __unaffected __alert	20. __thoughtful __fair-minded	29. __logical __adaptable
3. __cooperative __inventive	12. __sharp-witted __deliberate	21. __poised __ingenious	30. __sympathetic __patient
4. __friendly __cheerful	13. __kind __jolly	22. __sociable __steady	31. __stable __foresighted
5. __energetic __ambitious	14. __efficient __clear-thinking	23. __appreciative __good-natured	32. __honest __generous
6. __persevering __independent	15. __realistic __tactful	24. __pleasant __modest	33. __creative __altruistic
7. __loyal __dependable	16. __enterprising __intelligent	25. __responsible __reliable	34. __flexible __original
8. __determined __courageous	17. __affectionate __frank	26. __dignified __civilized	35. __scholarly __artistic
9. __industrious __practical	18. __progressive __thrifty	27. __imaginative __self-controlled	36. __confident __critical

In each of the pairs of words below check the one you think LEAST describes you.

37. __shy __lazy	46. __shallow __stingy	55. __despondent __evasive	64. __cynical __aggressive
38. __unambitious __reckless	47. __unstable __frivolous	56. __distractible __complaining	65. __dissatisfied __outspoken
39. __noisy __arrogant	48. __defensive __touchy	57. __weak __selfish	66. __undependable __resentful
40. __emotional __headstrong	49. __tense __irritable	58. __rude __self-centered	67. __sly __excitable
41. __immature __quarrelsome	50. __dreamy __dependent	59. __rattle-brained __disorderly	68. __irresponsible __impatient
42. __unfriendly __self-seeking	51. __changeable __prudish	60. __fussy __submissive	69. __compliant __cynical
43. __affected __moody	52. __nervous __intolerant	61. __opinionated __pessimistic	70. __tortuous __naive
44. __stubborn __cold	53. __careless __foolish	62. __shiftless __bitter	71. __conventional __impulsive
45. __conceited __infantile	54. __apathetic __egotistical	63. __hard-hearted __self-pitying	72. __conforming __inconsistent

Note: Items 33-36 and 69-72 are not part of the original Ghiselli Inventory. They were added for experimental purposes and are not considered in the trait scores reported in Chapter VI.

APPENDIX II

Statistical Treatment

Much of the information gathered for this study is in the form of discontinuous attributes rather than continuous series. Thus, much of the analysis is in terms of the percentage of subjects who display a given characteristic or who hold a certain opinion. To compare, say, major executives with minor executives, the difference between the percentages of subjects possessing the characteristic in question is the key factor. If a significantly greater proportion of one group than of the other exhibits an attribute, there is said to be some association between having this attribute and achieving a particular status in librarianship during the period covered by the subject, among these subjects, at least.

The tough question in the analysis of survey data is that of determining when a difference between two (or among three or more) percentages is "significant." The traditional method for assessing significance is to determine what the odds are that the difference might occur by mere chance. Arbitrary levels are selected (traditionally 95 to 1 or 99 to 1) for declaring that a difference is "significant" or "probably significant." This procedure has great value in evaluating the results of an experiment that is to be done only once, for example, the yield of two plots of ground treated with different fertilizers. However, statisticians have questioned the validity of using this method for picking out significant differences from a number of measures taken on the same subjects, as is the case in survey research. Since there are stochastic (chance) relationships not only between any two measurements but also among the various sets of observations, the rules of significance testing no longer hold. Lipset, Trow, and Coleman[1] discuss this and other difficulties involved in the use of significance tests, concluding:

...some factors...tend to make the test too weak, for they violate the assumptions on which the test is based.... On the other hand, there are certain factors which tend to make usual tests too strong; acceptance of the null hypothesis may occur even though a strong relationship does exist. Finally, there are serious questions about the relevance of such tests for analyses like this, even when they are neither too weak nor too strong.

For these reasons, many social survey agencies have abandoned the use of significance tests altogether. Others use them, with due regard for their limitations, on the theory that a crude measure, if it is a relevant one, is better than no measure at all. This is the point of view adopted here. It does seem useful to have an estimate of the odds against a relationship occurring merely by the cast of a die. One must remember that a test of significance refers only to the difference between two figures on a piece of paper and not to the factors that may have "caused" them to be different nor to the network of "prior" variables whose interaction may have canceled out, or intensified, one another and produced a spurious similarity between two figures in a table.[2]

For what they may be worth, simple standard-error tests of significance are reported in the course of this study. However, differences in the distribution of attributes among two or more groups will be discussed sometimes, even though these differences do not meet the customary .05 level of significance. In evaluating an hypothesis regarding differences between groups, one must avoid two types of error: Type I involves accepting an hypothesis of real difference when, in fact, the apparent difference is due merely to a chance variation. Type II error involves assigning an observed difference to chance when it actually represents a real difference. Rigid adherence to a given significance level may lead one into a Type II error in the process of avoiding a Type I.

Some of the data meet the requirements of parametric analysis. The same problems of multiple measurements as in nonparametric analysis of attributes are present here, but different and more precise methods are used in making the significance tests. Where data are in a continuous series (e.g., age or test scores), differences between means or other measures of central tendency may be computed and tested. For this, the technique known as analysis of variance has been used. Where comparison between information about attributes is to be compared with that for continuous variables, the continuous series may be treated as if they were attributes, e.g., one speaks of the "young" and the "old," or the "well

148   Appendix II

paid" and the "less well paid," or the "high scores" and the "lower scores."

The existence of association between two variables is one thing, the strength of that association is another. The traditional measure of the strength of the relationship between two continuous variables is the coefficient of correlation developed by Karl Pearson. It will be recalled that previous studies of librarians found rather low correlations between, say, grades in library school and salary received in later library positions. Inasmuch as most of the data collected for this study is not of the type to which Pearsonian correlation techniques are applicable, a nonparametric measure of association is used in the chapter on interrelations among variables. This measure, known as Yule's coefficient of association, is symbolized by "Q." It is a simple measure that is subject to the limitations discussed in Chapter V. As in the case of the more-familiar Pearsonian coefficient, Yule's Q approaches 1.00 when the association between two factors is great, and zero when they are unrelated. Technically speaking, it is a measure of predictability rather than dependence.[3]

To summarize: Statistical treatment has relied heavily on comparison of percentages of subjects possessing given characteristics or, in some cases, being on the high or low portion of a continuous scale. In cases where variables are normally distributed and continuous, analysis of variance was used. A simple index of association was reported in parts of the paper. Significance tests have been used sparingly and with due regard for their limitations when they are applied repeatedly to the same groups of data.

NOTES

[1] Seymour M. Lipset, Martin A. Trow, and James S. Coleman, *Union Democracy: The Internal Politics of the International Typographical Union* (Glencoe, Ill.: Free Press, 1956), p.428.

[2] Literature on this subject is reviewed and the argument against significance tests developed in Hanan C. Selvin, "A Critique of Tests of Significance in Survey Research," *American Sociological Review,* 22:519-27 (Oct. 1957). Use of tests in certain designs where adequate hypotheses have been developed prior to gathering data is defended in Leslie Kish, "Some Statistical Problems in Research Design," *ibid.,* 24:328-38 (June 1959).

[3] For further discussion of the problem of association, cf. Leo A. Goodman and William H. Kruskal, "Measures of Association for Cross Classifications," *Journal of the American Statistical Association,* 49:732-64 (Dec. 1954), and "Further Discussion and References," *ibid.,* 54:123-63 (March 1959).

APPENDIX III

Suggestions for Further Research

Virtually any of the factors (background, career, education, or personality) explored here could be the basis for more intensive study, using interview rather than questionnaire methods. The following approaches are suggested:

1. A sociometric study of librarians on two or more specific college or university campuses would be most enlightening. Such a detailed study of the administrative, professional, scholarly, organizational, and social contacts of academic librarians would provide a basis for estimating the seriousness of the *anomie,* or "lonely crowd," problem among librarians. If, say, four campuses were studied, two should be those on which librarians have academic rank and two on which they do not.

2. The persistent problem of the "iron law of oligarchy" as it affects professional organizations is in need of further study. Perhaps a study modeled after Lipset, Trow, and Coleman's *Union Democracy* is indicated.[1]

3. Research on library personnel is now far enough advanced for a longitudinal study to be feasible. For many purposes, studying the same group at two different points in time is more illuminating than studying different age groups at the same time. The time for a restudy of the subjects used by Douglass[2] in 1948 would seem to be nearly at hand. Or, in the manner of Warner and Abegglen's replication of Taussig's study of business leaders,[3] portions of the present study, of the Douglass investigation, or of the Public Library Inquiry could be repeated on a younger group to determine what changes have taken place since World War II.

4. A more detailed study of the self-perception pattern prevailing among librarians, using an integrated psychological and sociological approach, would seem to be in order. Such a study

149

would carry on the beginnings made by this and the Douglass study. Incidentally, the possibilities for study of the self-perception data gathered for the present survey have not been exhausted. The experimental items added to the original Ghiselli list of adjectives have not been analyzed. Such an analysis would shed light on the scholarly and aesthetic aspects of the librarian's personality, subjects not adequately covered by the Ghiselli list.

5. A study of the image of the academic librarian in the minds of other members of the academic community and of the general public could be a separate project or be done as parts of suggestions 1, 3, and 4.[4] Part of this inquiry might be an investigation of the reference-group perception of librarians. With whom, if anyone, do librarians compare themselves when they think about salary and status?

6. The changing pattern of social origin of librarians could be the subject of further inquiry. On the one hand, indications here are that such changes might become a source of psychological problems and social tensions among librarians. On the other hand, a broader social base is viewed as a source of democratic vigor for the ranks of the profession. Further testing of these hypotheses would seem to be indicated.

7. The charge of increasing anti-intellectualism among academic librarians, made by certain respondents to this survey, might be investigated. Such a study would investigate the effect, if any, on academic libraries and librarians of the waves of suspicion and distrust of unorthodoxy which seem to course through the mass society from time to time.[5]

8. A foundation-size project would be an extensive study of the effects of post-World War II changes in library education, perhaps after the manner of recent studies of business,[6] social work,[7] and medical[8] education. One aspect of such a study would be to evaluate the success of education for librarianship in providing for both uniformity and diversity. Has it prepared the wide variety of personnel needed for this encyclopedic profession and, at the same time, promoted a set of common ideals for librarianship as a distinct profession?

9. In all of the above studies, attention should be given to the effects of what appears to be a masculinization trend in academic librarianship and an evaluation made of means to utilize both man- and woman-power most effectively.

NOTES

[1] Seymour M. Lipset, Martin A. Trow, and James S. Coleman, *Union Democracy: The Internal Politics of the International Typographical Union* (Glencoe, Ill.: Free Press, 1956).

[2] Robert R. Douglass, "The Personality of the Librarian," (Ph.D. dissertation, Univ. of Chicago, 1957). (Microfilm)

[3] W. Lloyd Warner and James C. Abegglen, *Occupational Mobility in American Business and Industry, 1928-1952* (Minneapolis: Univ. of Minnesota Press, 1955).

[4] Robert D. Leigh and Kathryn Sewny, "The Popular Image of the Librarian," *Library Journal*, 85:2089-91 (June 1, 1960), and Gerhart Wiebe, "The Image: Its Definition and Measurement," *ibid.*, p.2092-97.

[5] Marjorie Fiske, *Book Selection and Censorship: A Study of School and Public Libraries in California* (Berkeley: Univ. of California Press, 1959).

[6] Robert A. Gordon and James E. Howell, *Higher Education for Business* (New York: Columbia Univ. Press, 1959), and Frank C. Pierson, *The Education of American Businessmen: A Study of University-College Programs in Business Administration* (New York: McGraw-Hill, 1959).

[7] Council on Social Work Education, *Comprehensive Report of the Curriculum Study* (New York: Council on Social Work Education, 1959). 13 vols.

[8] E.g., Kenneth R. Hammond, *et al.*, *Teaching Comprehensive Medical Care: A Psychological Study of a Change in Medical Education* (Cambridge, Mass.: For the Commonwealth Fund by Harvard Univ. Press, 1959), and Robert K. Merton, George G. Reader, and Patricia L. Kendall, eds., *The Student-Physician: Introductory Studies in the Sociology of Medical Education* (Cambridge, Mass.: For the Commonwealth Fund by Harvard Univ. Press, 1957).

Bibliography (TO 1960)

Books and Pamphlets

American Council on Education. *American Universities and Colleges*. Baltimore, Md.: Williams & Wilkins, 1932.

Anestasi, Anne. *Psychological Testing*. New York: Macmillan, 1954.

Asheim, Lester, comp. *The Core of Education for Librarianship*. A report of a workshop held under the auspices of the Graduate Library School of the University of Chicago, Aug. 10-15, 1953. Chicago: American Library Assn., 1954.

—— ed. *A Forum on the Public Library Inquiry*. New York: Columbia Univ. Press, 1950.

Barber, Bernard. *Social Stratification: A Comparative Analysis of Structure and Process*. New York: Harcourt, 1957.

Bendix, Reinhard, and Lipset, Seymour M., eds. *Class, Status and Power*. Glencoe, Ill.: Free Press, 1953.

Berelson, Bernard, ed. *Education for Librarianship*. Papers presented at the Library Conference, University of Chicago, Aug. 16-21, 1948. Chicago: American Library Assn., 1949.

Bisno, Herbert. *The Place of the Undergraduate Curriculum in Social Work Education* (A Project Report of the Curriculum Study, Vol. II). New York: Council on Social Work Education, 1959.

Blaustein, Albert P., and Porter, Charles O. *The American Lawyer: A Summary of the Survey of the Legal Profession*. Chicago: Univ. of Chicago Press, 1954.

---

*For subsequent references, consult footnotes for Chapter VII.

Bryan, Alice I. *The Public Librarian: A Report of the Public Library Inquiry.* New York: Columbia Univ. Press, 1952.

Caplow, Theodore, and McGee, Reece J. *The Academic Marketplace.* New York: Basic Books, 1958.

Caplow, Theodore. *The Sociology of Work.* Minneapolis: Univ. of Minnesota Press, 1954.

Carr-Saunders, Alexander M., and Wilson, P. A. *The Professions.* Oxford: Clarendon Press, 1933.

Carson, A. B. *The Public Accounting Profession in California: Report of the Findings of a Survey of the Profession: Its Practices and Its Personnel.* Los Angeles: Bureau of Business and Economic Research, Univ. of California, 1958.

Clark, Kenneth E. *America's Psychologists: A Survey of a Growing Profession.* Washington, D.C.: American Psychological Assn., 1957.

Commission on Human Resources and Advanced Training. *America's Resources of Specialized Talent: A Current Appraisal and a Look Ahead,* prepared by Dael Wolfle, director. New York: Harper, 1954.

Conference of College and University Librarians of Southern California. *Opportunities in College and University Librarianship.* N.p.: The Conference, 1949.

Consulting Engineer: Survey of the Profession. New York: Consulting Engineer, 1957.

Council on Social Work Education. *Comprehensive Report of the Curriculum Study.* New York: Council on Social Work Education, 1959. 13 vols.

Cuber, John F., and Kenkel, William F. *Social Stratification in the United States.* New York: Appleton, 1954.

Danton, J. Periam, ed. *The Climate of Book Selection: Social Influences on School and Public Libraries.* Papers presented at a symposium held at the University of California, July 10-12, 1958. Berkeley: Univ. of California School of Librarianship, 1959.

—— *Education for Librarianship: Criticisms, Dilemmas, and Proposals.* New York: School of Library Service, Columbia Univ., 1946.

Darley, John G., and Hagenah, Theta. *Vocational Interest Measurement, Theory and Practice.* Minneapolis: Univ. of Minnesota Press, 1955.

David, Lily M. *Economic Status of Library Personnel, 1949.* Chicago: American Library Assn., 1950.

Davis, Allison. *Deep South.* Chicago: Univ. of Chicago Press, 1941.

Davis, Kingsley. *Human Society*. New York: Macmillan, 1949.

Donovan, Frances R. *The Saleslady*. Chicago: Univ. of Chicago Press, 1929.

Durkheim, Emile. *Emile Durkheim on the Division of Labor in Society;* being a translation of his *De la division du travail social*, with an estimate of his work by George Simpson. New York: Macmillan, 1933.

Edwards, Alba M. *Comparative Occupational Statistics for the United States, 1870 to 1940*. Washington, D.C.: Govt. Print. Off., 1943.

—— *A Social-Economic Grouping of the Gainful Workers of the United States, Gainful Workers of 1930 in Social-Economic Groups, by Color, Nativity, Age, and Sex, and by Industry, with Comparative Statistics for 1920 and 1910*. Washington, D.C.: Govt. Print. Off., 1938.

Edwards, Allen L. *The Social Desirability Variable in Personality Assessment and Research*. New York: Dryden Press, 1957.

Eells, Kenneth. *Intelligence and Cultural Differences*. Chicago: Univ. of Chicago Press, 1951.

Fiske, Marjorie. *Book Selection and Censorship: A Study of School and Public Libraries in California*. Berkeley: Univ. of California Press, 1959.

Ginzberg, Eli. *Human Resources: The Wealth of a Nation*. New York: Simon & Schuster, 1958.

—— *et al. Occupational Choice: An Approach to a General Theory*. New York: Columbia Univ. Press, 1951.

Gordon, Milton M. *Social Class in American Sociology*. Durham, N. C.: Duke Univ. Press, 1958.

Gordon, Robert A., and Howell, James E. *Higher Education for Business*. New York: Columbia Univ. Press, 1959.

Harvey, John F. *Action Manual for Library Recruiters*. Reprinted from *Wilson Library Bulletin*, Vol. 31 (Sept., 1956).

—— *The Librarian's Career: A Study of Mobility* ("ACRL Microcard Series," No.85 [Rochester, N.Y.: Univ. of Rochester Press for the Assn. of College and Reference Libraries, 1957]).

Hughes, Everett C. *Men and Their Work*. Glencoe, Ill.: Free Press, 1958.

Knapp, Robert H., and Goodrich, H. B. *The Origins of American Scientists*. Middleton, Conn.: Wesleyan Univ., 1952.

—— and Greenbaum, J. J. *The Younger American Scholar: His Collegiate Origins*. Middleton, Conn.: Wesleyan Univ., 1953.

Lazarsfeld, Paul F. *The Academic Mind: Social Scientists in a Time of Crisis*. Glencoe, Ill.: Free Press, 1958.

Leigh, Robert D. *The California Librarian Education Survey: A Report to President Robert G. Sproul of the University of California.* New York: Columbia Univ., 1952.

Lewin, Kurt. *A Dynamic Theory of Personality.* New York: McGraw-Hill, 1935.

Lewis, Roy, and Maude, Angus. *Professional People.* London: Phoenix House, 1952.

Lieberman, Myron. *Education as a Profession.* Englewood Cliffs, N.J.: Prentice-Hall, 1956.

Lipset, Seymour M., and Bendix, Reinhard. *Social Mobility in Industrial Society.* Berkeley and Los Angeles: Univ. of California Press, 1959.

—— Trow, Martin A., and Coleman, James S. *Union Democracy: The Internal Politics of the International Typographical Union.* Glencoe, Ill.: Free Press, 1956.

Lyle, Guy R. *The Administration of the College Library.* 2d ed. rev. New York: Wilson, 1949.

Mack, Raymond; Freeman, Linton; and Yellin, Seymour. *Social Mobility: Thirty Years of Research and Theory.* New York: Syracuse Univ. Press, 1957.

Merton, Robert K., and Lazarsfeld, Paul F. *Continuities in Social Research: Studies in the Scope and Method of "The American Soldier."* Glencoe, Ill.: Free Press, 1950.

Merton, Robert K. *Social Theory and Social Structure.* Rev. ed. Glencoe, Ill.: Free Press, 1957.

—— Reader, George G., and Kendall, Patricia L., eds. *The Student-Physician: Introductory Studies in the Sociology of Medical Education.* Cambridge, Mass.: For the Commonwealth Fund by Harvard Univ. Press, 1957.

Mills, C. Wright. *White Collar.* New York: Oxford Univ. Press, 1951.

Moffett, M'ledge. *The Social Background and Activities of Teachers' College Students.* ("Teachers College Contribution to Education," No.375) New York: Teachers College, Columbia Univ., 1929.

Morse, Nancy C. *Satisfactions in the White-Collar Job.* Ann Arbor, Mich.: Survey Research Center, Institute for Social Research, Univ. of Michigan, 1953.

National Education Association. Educational Policies Commission. *Professional Organizations in American Education.* Washington, D.C.: National Education Assn., 1957.

National Manpower Council. *A Policy for Scientific and Professional Manpower.* New York: Columbia Univ. Press, 1953.

Newcomer, Mabel. *The Big Business Executive: The Factors*

That Made Him, 1900-1950. New York: Columbia Univ. Press, 1955.

Ostheimer, Richard H. *A Statistical Analysis of the Organization of Higher Education in the United States, 1948-49.* New York: Columbia Univ. Press, 1951.

Packard, Vance. *The Status Seekers: An Exploration of Class Behavior in America and the Hidden Barriers That Affect You, Your Community, Your Future.* New York: McKay, 1959.

Parsons, Algene. *Using Your Subject Major as a Special Librarian.* Pasadena, Calif.: Western Personnel Institute, 1959.

Pierson, Frank C. *The Education of American Businessmen: A Study of University-College Programs in Business Administration.* New York: McGraw-Hill, 1959.

Reagan, Agnes L. *A Study of Factors Influencing College Students To Become Librarians* ("ACRL Monograph," No.21) Chicago: Assn. of College and Research Libraries, American Library Assn., 1958.

Reece, Ernest J. *The Task and Training of Librarians;* a report of a field investigation carried out in February to May, 1947, to assist with curricular problems then pending before the Dean and Faculty at the School of Library Service, Columbia University. New York: King's Crown Press, 1949.

Reissman, Leonard. *Class in American Society.* Glencoe, Ill.: Free Press, 1959.

Robinson, Donald W. *Analysis of Motives for a Choice of a Teaching Career.* Philadelphia: Univ. of Pennsylvania, 1944.

Roe, Anne. *The Making of a Scientist.* New York: Dodd, 1953.

——— *The Psychology of Occupations.* New York: Wiley, 1956.

Rogoff, Natalie. *Recent Trends in Occupational Mobility.* Glencoe, Ill.: Free Press, 1953.

Rose, Arnold M. *Sociology: The Study of Human Relations.* New York: Knopf, 1956.

Rosenberg, Morris. *Occupations and Values.* Glencoe, Ill.: Free Press, 1957.

Ross, Ralph C., and Van den Haag, Ernest. *Fabric of Society.* New York: Harcourt, 1957.

Selznick, Philip. *Leadership in Administration: A Sociological Interpretation.* Evanston, Ill.: Row, Peterson, 1957.

Sorokin, Pitirim A. *Social Mobility.* New York: Harper, 1927.

Stagner, Ross. *The Psychology of Personality.* New York: McGraw-Hill, 1948.

Strong, Edward K., Jr. *Vocational Interests of Men and Women.* Stanford, Calif.: Stanford Univ. Press, 1943.

Stuit, Dewey B., *et al. Predicting Success in Professional Schools.* Washington, D.C.: American Council on Education, 1949.

Super, Donald E., and Bachrach, Paul B. *Scientific Careers and Vocational Development Theory: A Review, a Critique and Some Recommendations.* New York: Bureau of Publications, Teachers College, Columbia Univ., 1957.

Taussig, F. W., and Joslyn, C. S. *American Business Leaders.* New York: Macmillan, 1932.

Tyler, Leona E. *The Psychology of Human Differences.* 2d ed. New York: Appleton, 1956.

U.S. President's Commission on Higher Education. *Higher Education for American Democracy.* New York: Harper, 1947.

Visher, Stephen S. *Scientists Starred 1903-1943 in American Men of Science.* Baltimore, Md.: Johns Hopkins Univ. Press, 1947.

Warner, W. Lloyd. *American Life, Dream and Reality.* Chicago: Univ. of Chicago Press, 1953.

—— and Abegglen, James C. *Big Business Leaders in America.* New York: Harper, 1955.

—— *Occupational Mobility in American Business and Industry, 1928-1952.* Minneapolis: Univ. of Minnesota Press, 1955.

—— Meeker, Marchia, and Eells, Kenneth. *Social Class in America: A Manual of Procedure for the Measurement of Social Status.* Chicago: Science Research Associates, 1949.

—— Havighurst, Robert J., and Loeb, Martin B. *Who Shall Be Educated? The Challenge of Unequal Opportunities.* New York: Harper, 1944.

Weber, Max. *From Max Weber: Essays in Sociology,* trans., edited, and with an introduction by H. H. Gerth and C. Wright Mills. New York: Oxford Univ. Press, 1946.

Wheeler, Joseph L. *Progress and Problems in Education for Librarianship.* New York: Carnegie Corporation of New York, 1946.

Who's Who in Library Service. 2d ed. New York: Columbia Univ. Press, 1955.

Whyte, William H. *The Organization Man.* New York: Simon & Schuster, 1956.

Williamson, Charles C. *Training for Library Service: A Report Prepared for the Carnegie Corporation of New York.* New York, 1923.

Wilson, Logan. *The Academic Man.* New York: Oxford Univ. Press, 1942.

Wilson, Louis R., and Tauber, Maurice. *The University Library.* 2d ed. New York: Columbia Univ. Press, 1956.

Wittman, Milton. *Scholarship Aid in Social Work Education.* New York: Council on Social Work Education, 1956.

Wolfle, Dael. *See* Commission on Human Resources and Advanced Training.

Articles and Essays

Abrams, Albert J. "Barriers to the Employment of Older Workers," *Annals of the American Academy of Political and Social Science,* 279:62-71 (Jan. 1952).

"Academic Salaries, 1958-59: Report of Committee Z on the Economic Status of the Profession, "*AAUP Bulletin,* 45:157-94 (June 1959).

Adams, Stuart. "Origins of American Occupational Elites: 1900-1955," *American Journal of Sociology,* 62:360-68 (Jan. 1957).

—— "Real and Nominal Origins of Selected Occupational Elites," *Research Studies of the State College of Washington,* 23:121-29 (1955).

—— "Regional Differences in Vertical Mobility in a High Status Occupation," *American Sociological Review,* 15:228-35 (April 1950).

—— "Trends in Occupational Origins of Physicians," *American Sociological Review,* 18:404-9 (Aug. 1953).

Allen, Philip J. "Childhood Backgrounds of Success in a Profession," *American Sociological Review,* 20:186-90 (April 1955).

Anderson, Odin W. "The Sociologist and Medicine," *Social Forces,* 31:38-42 (Oct. 1952).

Bacon, Betty. "My Year in Library School—Some Second Thoughts," *Library Journal,* 84:1741-44 (June 1, 1959).

Bauer, Harry C. "Who Wants To Be a Librarian?" *ALA Bulletin,* 50:627-30 (Nov. 1956).

Becker, Howard S., and Carper, James W. "The Elements of Identification with an Occupation," *American Sociological Review,* 21:341-48 (June 1956).

—— "The Development of Identification with an Occupation," *American Journal of Sociology,* 61:289-98 (Jan. 1956).

Bendix, Reinhard; Lipset, Seymour M.; and Malm, Theodore. "Social Origins and Occupational Career Patterns," *Industrial and Labor Relations Review,* Vol.7 (Jan. 1954).

Benz, Dale M. "College and University Library Statistics, 1956-57," *College and Research Libraries,* 19:49-84 (Jan. 1958).

Blasingame, Ralph, Jr. "Placement," *Library Trends,* 3:22-31 (July 1954).

Blau, Peter M., *et al.* "Occupational Choice: A Conceptional Framework," *Industrial and Labor Relations Review,* 9:531-43 (July 1956).

Bond, H. M. "Productivity of National Merit Scholars by Occupational Class," *School and Society,* 85:267-68 (Sept. 28, 1957).

Bryan, Alice I. "Librarianship" in Douglas H. Fryer and Edwin R. Henry, eds., *Handbook of Applied Psychology,* Vol.II, p.638-43 New York: Rinehart, 1950. 2v.

Buerkle, Jack V. "Patterns of Socialization, Role, Conflict, and Leadership among Nurses," *Sociology and Social Research,* 44: 100-5 (Nov.-Dec. 1959).

Coates, Charles H., and Pellegrin, Roland J. "Executives and Supervisors: Contrasting Self-Conceptions and Conceptions of Each Other," *American Sociological Review,* 22:217-20 (April 1957).

Cogan, Morris L. "The Problem of Defining a Profession," *The Annals of the American Academy of Political and Social Science,* 297:105-11 (Jan. 1955).

Colton, George A. "Woman Administrators," *Library Journal,* 84: 1712 (June 1, 1959).

Dalton, Melville. "Informal Factors in Career Achievement," *American Journal of Sociology,* 56:407-15 (March 1951).

Danskin, David G. "Studies in the Sociological Aspects of Specific Occupations." *Personnel and Guidance Journal,* 36:104-11 (Oct. 1957).

Danton, J. Periam. "Doctoral Study in Librarianship in the United States," *College and Research Libraries,* 20:435-53 (Nov. 1959).

Davis, Beverly. "Eminence and Level of Social Origin," *American Journal of Sociology,* 59:11-18 (July 1953).

Devereux, George, and Weiner, Florence R. "The Occupational Status of Nurses," *American Sociological Review,* 15:628-34 (Oct. 1950).

Dibden, Arthur J. "Faculty, People and College Power," *AAUP Bulletin,* 40:529-36 (Dec. 1959).

Donnelly, J. R. "What Did They Do Then?" *ALA Bulletin,* 29:657-59 (Sept. 1935).

Downs, Robert B. "The Current Status of University Library Staffs," *College and University Libraries,* 18:375-85 (Sept. 1957).

—— "Distribution of American Library Resources," *College and Research Libraries,* 18:183-92 (May 1957).

Eckert, Ruth E.; Stecklein, John E.; and Sagen, Bradley. "College Faculty Members View Their Jobs," *AAUP Bulletin,* 45:513-28 (Dec. 1959).

Egan, Margaret E. "The Library and Social Structure," *Library Quarterly,* 25:15-22 (Jan. 1955).

Ellis, Evelyn. "Social Psychological Correlates of Upward Social Mobility of Unmarried Career Women," *American Sociological Review,* 47:558-63 (Oct. 1952).

"Fie, If Thy Name Be Woman" [Extract from the Preface to *Who's Who of American Women*. Chicago: Marquis, 1959], *Library Journal*, 84:556 (Feb. 15, 1959).

Freeman, Howard E.; Novak, Edwin; and Reeder, Leo G. "Correlates of Membership in Voluntary Associations," *American Sociological Review*, 22:528-33 (Oct. 1957).

Gaunt, Rezia. "Placement—To Be or Not To Be," *ALA Bulletin*, 48:84-88 (Feb. 1954).

Gee, Wilson. "Rural-Urban Origins of Leaders in Education," *Rural Sociology*, 2:402-8 (Dec. 1937).

Goode, William J. "Community within a Community: The Professions," *American Sociological Review*, 22:194-200 (April 1957).

Grasberger, Franz. "On the Psychology of Librarianship," *Library Quarterly*, 24:35-46 (Jan. 1954).

Gregory, Ruth W. "Illinois Looks at Recruiting: The Results of a Questionnaire," *Illinois Libraries*, 30:183-86 (May 1948).

Haer, John L. "Predictive Utility of Five Indices of Social Stratification," *American Sociological Review*, 22:541-46 (Oct. 1957).

Hall, Oswald. "Types of Medical Careers," *American Journal of Sociology*, 55:243-53 (Nov. 1949).

Harrison, Ross, *et al*. "A Profile of the Mechanical Engineer: I, Ability; II, Interests; III, Personality," *Personnel Psychology*, 8:219-34, 315-30, 469-90 (Summer, Autumn, Winter, 1955).

Harvey, John F. "Apply, If Thy Name Be Woman," *Library Journal*, 84:1712-13 (June 1, 1959).

—— "The Library School of the Future," *Library Journal*, 84:2433-36 (Sept. 1, 1959).

—— "Variety in the Experience of Chief Librarians," *College and Research Libraries*, 19:107-10 (March 1958).

Hatt, Paul K. "Stratification in the Mass Society," *American Sociological Review*, 15:216-22 (April 1950).

Heathcote, Lesley M. "More on Middle-Level Training," *Library Journal*, 84:2106 (July 1959).

Hintz, Carl W. "Personnel Administration—Discrimination, Despotism, Democracy," *PNLA Quarterly*, 16:15-24 (Oct. 1951).

Hoole, W. Stanley. "Of the Author-Librarian," *ALA Bulletin*, 47:161-65 (April 1953).

Howe, Harriet E. "Study of the University of Denver School of Librarianship Graduates, 1932-38," *Library Quarterly*, 10:532-44 (Oct. 1940).

—— "Traits of the Ideal and the Potential Librarian," *Library Quarterly*, 6:111-23 (April 1936).

—— "Two Decades in Education for Librarianship," *Library Quarterly*, 12:557-70 (July 1942).

Hyatt, Ruth. "Three Levels of Training," *Library Journal*, 84:660 (March 1, 1959).

Kent, Leonard R. "Economic Status of the Legal Profession in Chicago," *Illinois Law Review*, 45:311-32 (Jan.-Aug. 1950). (Summary of dissertation, Univ. of Chicago, 1950)

Knapp, Patricia B. "The College Librarian: Sociology of a Professional Specialization," *College and Research Libraries*, 16:66-72 (Jan. 1955).

—— Review of *A Study of Factors Influencing College Students To Become Librarians*, by Agnes Lyton Reagan. *Library Quarterly*, 29:152-53 (April 1959).

Komarovsky, Mirra. "The Voluntary Associations of Urban Dwellers," in Logan Wilson and William L. Kolb, eds., *Sociological Analysis*. New York: Harcourt, 1949. Originally appeared in *American Sociological Review*, 21:686-98 (Dec. 1946).

Kornhauser, Ruth R. "The Warner Approach to Social Stratification," in Reinhard Bendix and Seymour M. Lipset, *Class, Status, Power: A Reader in Social Stratification*. Glencoe, Ill.: Free Press, 1953.

Kraus, Joe W. "Qualifications of University Librarians," *College and Research Libraries*, 11:17-21 (Jan. 1950).

Labb, G. J. "Librarians in *Who's Who in America*," *Wilson Library Bulletin*, 25:54-56 (Sept. 1950).

Lenski, Gerhard E. "American Social Classes: Statistical Strata or Social Groups?," *American Journal of Sociology*, 58:139-44 (Sept. 1953).

Levin, Max M. "Status Anxiety and Occupational Choice," *Educational and Psychological Measurement*, 9:29-37 (Spring, 1949).

Lipset, Seymour M., and Malm, F. Theodore. "First Jobs and Career Patterns," *American Journal of Economics and Sociology*, 14:247-61 (April 1955).

—— and Trow, Martin. "Reference Group Theory and Trade Union Policy," in Mirra Komarovsky, ed., *Common Frontiers of the Social Sciences*. Glencoe, Ill.: Free Press, 1957.

—— and Bendix, Reinhard. "Social Mobility and Occupational Career Patterns: I, Stability of Jobholding; II, Social Mobility," *American Journal of Sociology*, 57:366-74, 494-504 (Jan. and Mar. 1952).

Marshall, T. H. "The Recent History of Professionalism in Relation to Social Structure and Social Policy," *The Canadian Journal of Economics and Political Science*, 5:335-40 (Aug. 1939).

McDiarmid, E. W. "Place of Experience in Developing College and University Librarians," *Library Quarterly*, 12:614-21 (July 1942).

McGuire, Carson. "Social Stratification and Mobility Pattern," *American Sociological Review*, 15:195-204 (April 1950).

North, Cecil C., and Hatt, Paul K. "Jobs and Occupations: a Popular Evaluation," in Logan Wilson and William L. Kolb,

Sociological Analysis, p.460. New York: Harcourt, 1949. Also appears in *Public Opinion News,* Sept. 1, 1947, p.3-13.

Ornsby, Lois. "If the Pay Is Good," *ALA Bulletin,* 54:356 (May 1960).

Pfautz, Harold W., and Duncan, Otis D. "A Critical Evaluation of Warner's Work in Community Stratification," *American Sociological Review,* 15:205-11 (April 1950).

Pinneau, Samuel R., and Milton, Alexander. "The Ecological Veracity of the Self-Report," *Journal of Genetic Psychology,* 93:249-76 (Dec. 1958).

Porter, Lyman W. "Differential Self-Perceptions of Management Personnel and Line Workers," *Journal of Applied Psychology,* 42:105-8 (April 1958).

Powell, Benjamin E. "A Help and Ornament Thereunto," *ALA Bulletin,* 53:685-88, 722 (Sept. 1959).

Rapoport, Lydia. "In Defense of Social Work: An Examination of Stress in the Profession," *The Social Service Review,* 34:62-74 (March 1960).

Reiss, A. J., Jr. "Occupational Mobility of Professional Workers," *American Sociological Review,* 20:693-700 (Dec. 1955).

Rettig, Salmon; Jacobson, F. N.; and Pasamanick, B. "Status Overestimation: Objective Status and Job Satisfaction among Professionals," *American Sociological Review,* 23:75-81 (Feb. 1958).

Rose, Arnold M. "Incomplete Socialization," *Sociology and Social Research,* 44:244-50 (March-April 1960).

Scott, John C., Jr. "Membership and Participation in Voluntary Associations," *American Sociological Review,* 22:315-26 (June 1957).

Shaffer, Kenneth R. "Personnel and the Library School," *Library Trends,* 3:13-21 (July 1954).

Sjoberg, Gideon. "Are Social Classes in America Becoming More Rigid," *American Sociological Review,* 21:775-78 (Dec. 1951).

Skipper, James E. "The Library Student Speaks," *Association of American Library Schools Newsletter,* 2:12-14 (Jan. 1950).

Slocum, W. L. "Some Sociological Aspects of Occupational Choice," *American Journal of Economics and Sociology,* 18:139-47 (Jan. 1959).

Smith, Harvey L. "Contingencies of Professional Differentiation," *American Journal of Sociology,* 63:410-14 (Jan. 1958).

Stewart, Lawrence H. "Certain Factors Related to the Occupational Choices of Experienced Teachers," *Peabody Journal of Education,* 33:235-39 (Jan. 1956).

Stogdill, Ralph M. "Personal Factors Associated with Leadership: A Survey of the Literature," *Journal of Psychology,* 25:35-71 (Jan. 1948).

Bibliography 163

Stryker, Perrin. "On the Meaning of Executive Qualities," *Fortune*, 57:116-19, 186-89 (June 1958).

Sussman, Leila A. "The Personnel and Ideology of Public Relations," *Public Opinion Quarterly*, 12:697-708 (Winter, 1948-49).

Taylor, M. Lee, and Pellegrin, Roland J. "Professionalization: Its Functions and Dysfunctions for the Life Insurance Occupation," *Social Forces*, 38:110-14 (Dec. 1959).

Thorner, Isidor. "Nursing: The Functional Significance of an Institutional Pattern," *American Sociological Review*, 20:531-38 (Oct. 1955).

Threlkeld, Curtis H. "Problems in the Recruitment and Adjustment of Teachers," *Bulletin of the National Association of Secondary School Principals*, 32:169-75 (March 1948).

Van Zelst, R. H., and Kerr, W. A. "Personality Self-Assessment of Scientific and Technical Personnel," *Journal of Applied Psychology*, 38:145-47 (June 1954).

Visher, Stephen S. "Environmental Backgrounds of Leading American Scientists," *American Sociological Review*, 13:65-72 (Feb. 1948).

Wardwell, Walter I., and Wood, Arthur L. "The Extra-Professional Role of the Lawyer," *American Journal of Sociology*, 61:304-7 (Jan. 1956).

Willhelm, Sidney, and Sjoberg, Gideon. "The Social Characteristics of Entertainers," *Social Forces*, 37:71-76 (Oct. 1958).

Williams, Josephene J. "Patients and Prejudice: Lay Attitudes Toward Women Physicians," *American Journal of Sociology*, 51:283-87 (Jan. 1946).

Williams, Lloyd P. "The Pariah Status of the Teacher," *Education*, 74:261-63 (Dec. 1953).

Wilson, Eugene H. "Pre-Professional Background of Students in a Library School," *Library Quarterly*, 8:157-88 (April 1938).

Wilson, Louis R. "The Objectives of the Graduate Library School in Extending the Frontiers of Librarianship," in *New Frontiers of Librarianship*, p.13-26. Chicago: Graduate Library School, Univ. of Chicago, 1940.

Wilson, V. W. "Some Personality Characteristics of Industrial Executives," *Occupational Psychology*, 30:228-31 (Oct. 1956).

Winslow, Amy. "Supervision and Morale," *Library Trends*, 3:39-51 (July 1954).

Reports of Corporate Bodies

American Library Association. Association of College and Reference Libraries. College and University Postwar Planning Committee. *College and University Libraries and Librarianship*. Chicago: A.L.A., 1946.

—— Board of Education for Librarianship. "The Librarian [Report for 1947-48]," *ALA Bulletin*, 42:445-47 (Oct. 15, 1948).

—— "Standards for Accreditation," *ALA Bulletin*, 46:48-49 (Feb. 1952).

—— Board on Personnel Administration. Subcommittee on Analysis of Library Duties. "Descriptive List of Professional and Nonprofessional Duties in Libraries." Preliminary Draft. Chicago: A.L.A., 1948. (Mimeographed)

—— Committee on Accreditation. "Standards and Guide for Undergraduate Library Science Programs," *ALA Bulletin*, 52:695-700 (Oct. 1958).

—— Committee on Recruiting for Library Service. "Recruiting for Library Service [Annual Report of the Committee]," *ALA Bulletin*, 24:165-66 (May 1930).

Association of American Library Schools. Committee on Recruiting Personnel. "Why Library School Students Chose the Library Profession." 1953. (Mimeographed)

National Education Association. Research Division. *Economic Status of Teachers in 1958-59*. Washington, D.C.: National Education Assn., 1959.

—— —— *Salaries Paid and Salary Practices in Universities, Colleges, and Junior Colleges, 1959-60*. (Research Report, 1960, R 3) Washington, D.C.: National Education Assn., 1960.

Unpublished or Quasi-Published Material

Alvarez, Robert S. "Qualifications of Public Librarians in the Middle West. A Dissertation Submitted to the Faculty of the Graduate Library School . . . in Candidacy for the Degree of Doctor of Philosophy [Univ. of Chicago], 1939." Chicago: 1943. (Mimeographed)

Berninghausen, David K., ed. "Undergraduate Library Education: Standards, Accreditation, Articulation. Proceedings of the Institute on Undergraduate Library Education, October 31-November 1, 1958." Minneapolis: 1959. (Mimeographed)

Borenstein, Audrey F. "The Ethical Ideal of the Professions: A Sociological Analysis of the Academic and Medical Professions" (Doctoral dissertation, Dept. of Sociology, Louisiana State Univ., 1958), *Dissertation Abstracts*, 19:589-90 (Sept. 1958).

Danton, J. Periam, and Merritt, LeRoy C. "Characteristics of the Graduates of the University of California School of Librarianship." (Univ. of Illinois Library School, "Occasional Papers," No.22, June 1951) (Mimeographed)

Douglass, Robert R. "The Personality of the Librarian." Ph.D. dissertation, Univ. of Chicago, 1957. (Microfilm)

—— "The Personality of the Librarian." Dissertation abstract, Graduate Library School, Univ. of Chicago, 1957. (Mimeographed)

Emerich, Paul H. "The Background, Experience, Present Status and Self-Appraisal of the College Teacher of Education in Michigan" (Ph.D. dissertation, Univ. of Michigan, 1957), *Dissertation Abstracts,* 18:1346 (April 1958).

Ghiselli, Edwin E. "Self-Description Inventory." Univ. of California, 1957. (Processed)

Hoage, Althea A. "Job History of a Library School Class, 1937-1949." Atlanta Univ., May 1950. (Processed)

Imse, Thomas P. "The Professionalization of Business Management in Real Estate Firms" (Ph.D. dissertation, Univ. of Maryland, 1958), *Dissertation Abstracts,* 19:188 (July 1958).

James, Warren E. "Differential Acceptance of Occupations as Professions" (Ph.D. dissertation, Ohio State Univ., 1957), *Dissertation Abstracts,* 17:1620 (July 1957).

Metzger, Paul L. "An Investigation of Some Correlates of Vocational Interest Similarity between Fathers and Sons." Ph.D. dissertation, Univ. of Oregon, 1958.

Milczewski, Marion A. "Personality Rating of Library School Students." Master's thesis, Univ. of Illinois, 1940. (Microfilm)

Richardson, Stephen Alexander. "A Study of Selected Personality Characteristics of Social Science Field Workers" (Ph.D. dissertation, Cornell Univ., 1954), *Dissertation Abstracts,* 14:2403-4 (Dec. 1954).

Strauss, Samuel. "Backgrounds and Traits of a Group of Biological and Social Scientists" (Ph.D. dissertation, Univ. of Maryland, 1955), *Dissertation Abstracts,* 16:707-8 (April 1956).

University of California. Public Information—Radio. "Who's the Boss?" (University Explorer Broadcast, No.1542, April 28, 1957) (Mimeographed)

Welch, Ellsworth. "Motivational Factors in Choice of Profession by American Scientists" (Ed.D. dissertation, Stanford Univ., 1959), *Dissertation Abstracts,* 20:1233-34 (Oct. 1959).